D0169354

WITHDRAWAL

Understanding Creativity in Early Childhood

Understanding Creativity in Early Childhood

Meaning-Making and Children's Drawings

Susan Wright

Los Angeles | London | New Delhi
Singapore | Washington DC

SAGE Publications Ltd
1 Oliver's Yard
55 City Road
London EC1Y 1SP

SAGE Publications Inc.
2455 Teller Road
Thousand Oaks, California 91320

SAGE Publications India Pvt Ltd
B 1/I 1 Mohan Cooperative Industrial Area
Mathura Road
New Delhi 110 044

SAGE Publications Asia-Pacific Pte Ltd
33 Pekin Street #02-01
Far East Square
Singapore 048763

Library of Congress Control Number 2009932425

British Library Cataloguing in Publication data

A catalogue record for this book is available from
the British Library

ISBN 978-1-84787-525-9
ISBN 978-1-84787-526-6 (pbk)

Typeset by C&M Digitals (P) Ltd., Chennai, India
Printed in Great Britain by MPG Group, Bodmin, Cornwall
Printed on paper from sustainable resources

Mixed Sources
Product group from well-managed
forests and other controlled sources
www.fsc.org Cert no. SA-COC-1565
© 1996 Forest Stewardship Council

FSC

This book is dedicated to the children who generously shared their visual narratives about the future.

Contents

Acknowledgements   viii
About the Author   ix
List of Figures and Tables   x

1 Creativity: Meaning-Making and Representation   1

2 Surfacing the Voices of Children: The Role of the Interlocutor   25

3 Intratextuality in Drawing-Telling   53

4 Drawing and Embodiment   77

5 Intertextuality: Borrowing with a Personal Stamp   109

6 Ancient Forms → New Worlds   137

7 Implications for Teaching   165

References   179
Author Index   185
Subject Index   186

Acknowledgements

This project received Queensland University of Technology funding. Diane Reardon, Kathleen Rundell and Barbara Piscitelli were members of the research team in the early stages of the project and provided me with deeper insights into Futures Studies, helped compile the photographs and shape the direction of the pre-data collection discussions with the children, gave me access to and liaised with the schools and assisted in training the interlocutor. Gratitude is expressed to the interlocutor, Leslie Abbot, for her tireless and sensitive interactions with the children, and to the transcribers for their meticulous viewing of video footage and capturing of narrative, graphic and embodied content: Elizabeth Ayres, Merindy Shield, Felicity McArdle, Rekka Sharma and Mirjana Ristovski. Appreciation is extended to Deb Brown who learned N-Vivo, set up the initial parameters for coding and participated in some of the early data analysis to trial the software.

Special gratitude is extended to Felicity McArdle, Barbara Piscitelli and Madonna Stinson for their insights through the lenses of arts teachers, researchers and academics, and for their continued friendship, support, intellectual debate and appreciation of life over the many years of our friendship. I am deeply appreciative of the advice and support given to me by Shirley Brice-Heath, Courtney Cazden, Stephanie Burridge, John Matthews and Jeannette Bopry in helping me think about aspects of semiotics, multimodality and artistic literacy. And lastly, but most importantly, I thank my husband Joachim Diederich for his continuous love, support and belief in all that I do and everything that I might become.

About the Author

Susan Wright is Professor of Early Childhood Education at the National Institute of Education, Nanyang Technological University, Singapore. Formerly she was Director of the Centre for Applied Studies in Early Childhood at the Queensland University of Technology in Brisbane, Australia.

Her research and teaching interests include children's creativity and multimodal learning, arts pedagogy and developmental semiotics. She has undertaken several research projects which focus on issues such as young children's cross-modal interpretation of emotion in art and music, the transition of early childhood ideologies into lower primary school teachers' pedagogy, and creativity and representational practices in arts domains and school pedagogy. Her publications include *The Arts, Young Children and Learning, Special Education Perspectives and Practices* and *Children, Meaning-Making and the Arts* (which currently is being developed as a second edition) and numerous articles on early childhood education.

List of Figures and Tables

Figures

1.1	Lifting Off from Earth (boy, 6.6)	1
1.2	Olympic Equestrian Event (girl, 7.9)	16
2.1	Interlocutor with Child	25
2.2	Time Machine (boy, 8.5)	33
2.3	Surveillance System [detail] (boy, 8.2)	35
2.4	Police Officer Catching Baddies (girl, 5.7)	37
2.5	Walking on Sharp Rocks (girl, 5.0)	38
2.6	Having a Baby (girl, 5.7)	39
2.7	Fairy and Secret Garden (girl, 5.0)	42
2.8	Driver Training (boy, 5.9)	44
2.9	Family Picnic (boy, 5.8)	48
3.1	Cat, Dog, Mop and Mill (boy, 5.3)	53
3.2	Me, Parents and Dog (boy, 5.4)	58
3.3	Rainforest, Cloud and Bird (girl, 6.3)	58
3.4	North Brisbane Roadworks (boy, 5.7)	59
3.5	Reuban Backhoeing (boy, 5.2)	60
3.6	Multiple Drawings (girl, 8.2)	62
3.7a	Descending Sun Rays [detail] (girl, 8.0)	63
3.7b	Ascending Heat Rays [detail] (boy, 9.0)	63
3.8	Car Whoosh Lines (boy, 4.8)	64
3.9	Swimming with Sister (girl, 8.6)	65
3.10	Trampolining (girl, 5.0)	66
3.11	Horse Riding (girl, 8.3)	66
3.12	Mother, Children and Cat (girl, 5.0)	68
3.13	Friends Together (girl, 6.0)	69
3.14	Family and Possessions (boy, 5.0)	69
3.15	Bride in Church (girl, 6.0)	70
3.16	Living on Other Planets (girl, 7.8)	72
4.1	Shooting a Criminal (boy, 7.8)	77
4.2	Tumbling Blocks (boy, 5.2)	79
4.3	Koala Crossing the Road (girl, 6.0)	85
4.4	Remote Control Car (boy, 5.4)	88
4.5	In the Flood with Love Hearts (girl, 4.7)	89
4.6	Me, Mum, Diamond and Waterfall (boy, 5.0)	92
4.7	In Space in a Rocket (boy, 5.4)	93
4.8	Robbing a House (boy, 8.5)	98

4.9   Ant and Worm Houses [detail] (boy, 6.7)   100
4.10 The Future Rock Star (boy, 6.5)   101
4.11 Working in an Office with Swiveling Chair (girl, 5.8)   102
4.12 Olympic Medalists (boy, 8.0)   104
4.13 The City (girl, 8.7)   105
4.14 Mr Grouch's Castle (boy, 8.0)   105

5.1   Semi-Taxi and Sky Patrol (boy, 8.0)   109
5.2   Mowing the Lawn (boy, 6.0)   115
5.3   Chasing the Dog (girl, 5.5)   115
5.4   Road Workers Waving (boy, 6.0)   116
5.5   Blind Man with Dog (girl, 6.0)   116
5.6   Storyboarded Events   117
5.7   Crane Drivers (boy, 5.7)   119
5.8   The Olympics and the Police Place (boy, 6.4)   120
5.9   Fading the Sun In, Out and In Again [detail]   121
5.10 Dogs Running Over Slide [detail]   123
5.11 Frames for Theme-Based Sequences [details]   123
5.12 Policeman and Dog Chasing Criminal [detail]   124
5.13 Ethan and TJ Chasing Pig [detail]   125
5.14 Leaving Home [detail]   125

6.1   New Planet in 5000 (boy, 8.5)   137
6.2   Dual Parks and Pollution (boy, 8.1)   141
6.3   Magic Birds and Special Animals (boy, 6.3)   145
6.4   Family in Spaceship (girl, 6.2)   146
6.5   Beyond 2050 (boy, 6.6)   147
6.6   Singing in the Stadium (girl, 8.3)   153
6.7   The Magic Story (girl, 6.1)   156
6.8   Living, Dying, Evolution and War (girl, 8.5)   157
6.9   The Future at Mars (boy, 7.8)   160
6.10 The Sunrise of Life (girl, 8.5)   161

7.1   Houses and Drawings (girl, 5.5)   165

Tables

1.1   Creative Processes, Descriptions and Examples   5
1.2   Modes and Features of Meaning in Visual Narratives   21

4.1   Configuration, Movement, Language:
      Backhoeing, Stepping   91
4.2   Function, Form, Purpose: Connection, Separation   100
4.3   Mode, Form, Function: Enactive, Iconic, Symbolic   106

1

Creativity:
Meaning-Making and Representation

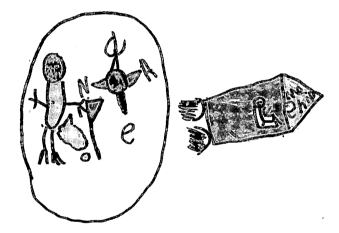

Figure 1.1 Lifting Off from Earth (boy, 6.6 i.e. 6 years, 6 months)

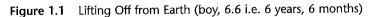

At the completion of this chapter, you should be able to:

1. Describe the important role of drawing in promoting creativity and meaning-making in young children,
2. Understand graphic, narrative and embodied aspects of children's meaning-making and representation, and
3. Reflect on how the content of a child's drawing is closely related to the form in which it is created.

Art and learning

The imagination is energetically deployed and reaches its peak in children's early years of life, however, it gradually declines as children grow order. Yet as Egan (1999) urges, imagination is precisely what is needed to keep us intellectually flexible and creative in modern societies. Most notably, the arts 'play to the imagination' (Gadsden, 2008, p. 47). Gadsden elaborates that the arts:

> allow individuals to place themselves in the skin of another; to experience others' reality and culture; to sit in another space; to transport themselves across time, space, era in history, and context; and to see the world from a different vantage point. (p. 35)

Arts education and early childhood education in general have emphasized important principles that have increasingly found their way into more recent studies on multimodality and new literacies. Such studies have opened up debates about what 'counts as a text and what constitutes reading and writing' and have extended our notions of creativity (Hull & Nelson, 2005, p. 224). For decades, early childhood educators, artists and arts educators have recognized that the arts draw upon a variety of modalities, such as speech, image, sound, movement and gesture, to create multimodal forms of meaning. Such experiences are fundamental to the fluidity and flexibility of human thought and learning. Art provides young people with authentic meaning-making experiences that engage their minds, hearts and bodies.

This book focuses on how young children's creativity is surfaced through the act of meaning-making within the medium of drawing. As will be illustrated through many examples of children's works, drawing is an imaginative act which involves a range of creative forms of sign production and interpretation. Like all areas of learning, becoming competent in drawing generally requires exposure, participation and practice. It is when there is refined mastery of an art medium, combined with high levels of creativity and talent, that breakthroughs can be accomplished, such as in the case of Picasso. Picasso was an outstanding individual who showed exceptional artistic ability at an early age (Gardner, 1993a), and continued to develop his expertise throughout his life.

In a sense, every instance of representation through art is new and creative. Although drawing involves a 'set of rules', children never just mechanically apply rules when they make an artwork. Generally, each artwork is different and requires adaptation to the circumstances at hand. This is why composing through art is such an important and fundamental form of creativity.

Creativity

Several authors have written extensively on the topic of creativity. This literature will not be described in detail here, as the focus is on illustrating how creativity is demonstrated in young children's art-making processes. However, some fundamental issues are featured at this time, and examples throughout this book will illustrate these, with a particular focus on meaning-making and representation through drawing.

Let us begin with a brief definition of creativity. Creativity is the process of generating ideas that are novel and bringing into existence a product that is appropriate and of high quality (Sternberg & Lubart, 1995). Everyone has at least some creative potential, but they differ widely in the extent to which they are able to realise that potential. In addition, as Gardner (1983, 1993a, b) pointed out, people tend to be creative or intelligent in some specific domains but not necessarily in others. For instance, we might be good at art, but not music; or be good at science, but not maths.

This is because creativity is a cognitive or *mental trait* and a *personality trait* as well. Some personal qualities include (Wright, 2003a): a valuing of creativity, originality, independence, risk-taking, the ability to redefine problems, energy, curiosity, attraction to complexity, artistry, open-mindedness, a desire to have some time alone, perceptiveness, concentration, humour, the ability to regress and the possession of childlike qualities. These personality traits are linked to thinking styles, which involve: visualization, imagination, experimentation, analogical/metaphorical thinking, logical thinking, predicting outcomes or consequences, analysis, synthesis and evaluation. In addition, intrinsic motivation and commitment are important personal qualities that are fundamental to the development of creativity.

Creative individuals were once widely seen as receiving divine inspiration for their ingenuity, and as needing nothing or anyone to excel. The stereotype is of a born genius whose innate talent does not require further honing or the support of others. Yet, in reality, the role of others is crucial throughout creative individuals' development (Perkins, 1981). Creative activity grows out of the relationships between an individual, his/her work in a discipline and the ties between the individual and other people (or institutions) who judge the quality of his/her work (Csikszentmihalyi, 1988).

Hence, teachers, parents and the community influence children's participation and development, and can support (or alternatively thwart) their creativity. Indeed, the decision to encourage or limit creativity is related to the attitudes of the significant people who shape children's environments – whether they value creativity and are tolerant of the children's ideas or products, even if these may challenge their own viewpoints or digress from conventional thinking and behaving.

Creativity is closely tied to personal connection, expression, imagination and ownership. It involves problem *setting* as well as problem *solving*. It comes out of explicit probing into meaningful issues, and constructing meaningful interpretations. Meaningful art-making reflects the ways of thinking of young artists – the makers who actively interact with the artwork. John Dewey (1934/1988) suggests that art offers multiple entry-points into the aesthetic experience, combining creation and appreciation. Indeed, children's early representational drawings often emerge as a result of a dialogue between production and perception (Thompson, 1995; Thompson & Bales, 1991).

The imagination of the child can transform a blank piece of paper into something very real. Young children are careful planners during the creative process of drawing. They often decide in advance what content is to be included and where to locate it on the page. Frequently they review their work-in-progress and make additions or corrections. Golomb (2004, p. 191) emphasizes that composition in art is an ongoing process of revision, of 'monitoring the performance, planning actions, inspecting the outcome, deciding on its merits and flaws'.

Although there are numerous ways in which creativity can evolve, some key processes are described in Table 1.1, along with an illustrative example of how these might apply to the medium of drawing. I am somewhat reluctant to introduce a range of technical terms, because these may seem to merely serve as a list or be viewed as being exhaustive rather than illustrative. Rather, the aim is to aid debate; by labelling some of the distinctive features of creativity in relation to drawing, allowing some security in the discussion. For a more extensive elaboration on some of these issues, readers may like to refer to some of my earlier works, particularly *The Arts, Young Children and Learning* (Wright, 2003a).

Artistic creation, through the medium of drawing, enables children to improvise. In the process, they develop a sense of arrangement and structure while transforming their graphic content on the blank page. This creative process is liberated through open-ended composing.

Table 1.1   Creative Processes, Descriptions and Examples

Creative process	Description	Example
Problem finding and solving	Finding and exploring alternative goals and approaches to a problem	Blending yellow, orange and brown to create the desired colour for a drawn dog's fur
Flexibility	Taking different approaches to a problem, thinking of ideas in a variety of ways or viewing a problem from another perspective	Changing a daytime scene into night by scribbling out a drawn yellow sun
Fluency	Producing many free-flowing ideas for an open-ended problem or question	Illustrating different unfolding events that flow in and out of the overall plot scheme of the drawing
Elaboration	Adding details to an idea, which includes developing, embellishing and improving the idea	Verbally explaining how a drawn object, such as a car, 'moves' across the page to get to the other side, or adding a wavy line to show the path of the movement
Transformation	Changing one object or idea into another by adding, subtracting, substituting or transposing	Noting that a drawn cloud looks like a shark, and adding details to make it into a 'flying shark'
Objectivity and selectivity	Going beyond generating ideas to distinguishing which of these ideas are the best and worth pursing	Choosing the 'best' colours, shapes or lines to depict something and deciding where to locate it on the page
Aesthetic appreciation	Striving for something which has purpose, results and high standards	Carefully detailing graphic content so that it communicates clearly and elegantly

Composing through drawing

Bresler (2002, p. 172) described Child Art as 'original, open-ended (in at least some aspects) compositions which are intended to reflect students' interpretations and ideas'. While composing, children are comfortable with altering their artworks to suit their purpose. They feel at liberty to improvise structures as they dialogue with the materials, such as changing birds to butterflies, scribbling out a dead figure or turning grass into water. A number of things may stimulate a child to improvise in ways such as these, which may include:

- changing the identity of a *character* (e.g., deciding that a prototypic rock star in a drawing should be the artist himself)
- altering the *plot* content (e.g., modifying the structure of the plot by introducing a new theme, scene or event)

- modifying the *genre* of the narrative (e.g., shifting from factual to fictional)
- adjusting the *time* frame (e.g., shifting between the present, future or past)
- varying the *place* (e.g., turning a house into a hotel)
- confronting a challenging *schema* (e.g., leaving 'Daddy' out of a family scene because the artist does not know how to draw men's clothes), or
- seeing another *image* in what has been drawn (e.g., thinking that a drawn dog looks more like a bear, and adding salient content to refine the image).

Most children seem to find composing through art an appealing process, perhaps because it is not strictly *rule-bound*. Children are at liberty to experiment and to represent ideas and actions in whatever form they choose. Hence, my intention is to feature not just the *content* of children's artworks, but to also emphasize how the *form* of this content is meaningful. I want to highlight how children's art making is an active, meaning-making experience. Like Kress (1997), I take the position that children's visual narrative texts have structure, and that the structure that is given to these texts is done so through the interests of the text makers. It is a transformative process. The signs that children make are different from adult forms, but nonetheless, they are fully meaningful.

Art allows children to 'say' and 'write' what they think and feel, usually without adult intrusion. Through such open-ended experiences, children develop a repertoire of marks, images and ideas. They refine these through practice and skill and through exposure to the art of other children and adults. In the process, children experiment with 'the language' of the materials and develop a 'grammar' of communication. As mentioned above, they decide not only on the *content* to be depicted, but also the aesthetic *form*, or the manner in which content is presented. The artwork's compositional component is a vital element of the child's communication. It is the organizational force used to project ideas and to illustrate relativity and relationships. Composition not only makes the content accessible, it also heightens the young artist's perceptions and stimulates his or her imaginative involvement.

When composing through drawing, children combine graphic, narrative and embodied signs. Dyson (1993) noted that at around the age of two, children often use drawing as a prop for storytelling, complemented with dramatic gesture and speech. These multimodal texts involve drawing, gesture and talk – they stem from visual, linguistic, aural and tactile modes to make meaning. Indeed, the marks that children make are often the 'visual equivalent of dramatic play' (Anning, 1999, p. 165).

Because of the play-oriented, compositional component of drawing, I believe art is essentially the *literacy par excellence* of the early years of child development (Wright, 2007b). As many have noted, infants and very young children generally draw *prior* to the acquisition of the skills of reading and writing written text (i.e., letters, words, phrases, sentences). Gunther Kress, in his book *Before Writing* (1997, p. 10), describes the social, cultural and cognitive implications of the 'transition from the rich world of meanings made in countless ways, in countless forms, in the early years of children's lives, to the much more unidimensional world of written language'.

Indeed, the act of representing thought and action while drawing actually strengthens children's later understanding of literacy and numeracy. Unfortunately, however, many traditional systems of schooling suppress children's *free composing* through drawing in favour of *teaching* children the more rule-bound, structured symbol systems of numeracy and literacy. This is because schools often perceive writing letters, words and numbers as a 'higher status' mode of representation (Anning & Ring, 2004). Yet, as Pahl and Rowsell (2005, p. 43) noted, many children are constrained by a literacy curriculum that only allows writing. They asserted that a multimodal approach 'lets in more meaning'.

To focus too strongly, too soon, on a literacy curriculum distracts children from the ability to compose using pictorial signs, which in many ways are developmentally more meaningful to young children. When picturing and imagining within the 'fluid' boundaries of art, children are in control of *what* they want to say and *how* they want to say it, in a free-form way. The less rule-bound system of drawing offers children freedom of 'voice'. When this co-exists with the learning of the more structured symbol systems, children engage in creative meaning-making in an assortment of ways.

Composing through art, like play, is a fundamental function of early cognitive, effective and social development. Through art, children actively *construct* understandings of themselves and their worlds, rather than simply becoming the passive recipients of knowledge. To suppress and replace artistic play with formal teaching not only denies the voice of children, but overlooks the significance of composing in the act of meaning construction.

Yet, Kress emphasized that, perhaps in the absence of strong theoretical descriptions and explanations of art, drawings and images of most kinds are thought of as being about expression, rather than about information or communication. Hence, art is not usually subjected to the same analysis for meaning, or seen as being as important a part of communication as language (Kress, 1997, p. 35). Kress adds that if the makers of the artworks are children, the question of 'intentionality and design becomes contentious' (Kress, 1997, p. 36).

The goal of this book is to overcome some of these misconceptions by providing a theoretical foundation for understanding and appreciating the artworks that stemmed from the participation of over 100 5–8-year-old Australian children. The children were asked to draw and talk about what the future will be like, on a one-to-one basis, with a trained interlocutor, who interacted with each child throughout the process (an aspect which will be described in greater detail in Chapter 2).

The topic 'Futures' was chosen to inspire children to break out of the common schemata (e.g., trees, houses, the sun) that often are inherent in self-selected, rehearsed drawings. Indeed, it was found that this topic stimulated children to mentally manipulate and organize images, ideas and feelings about complex subjects, and to engage in a rich amalgam of both fantasy and reality. It inspired children to speculate on futures yet to come – to consider multiple interpretations, to generate new meanings and to expand existing ones. Such thinking involves a high-order consciousness (Slaughter, 1994b). It also appeals to children's interest in things that are far from what they know firsthand, such as aliens, spaceships, force-fields and virtual reality.

This propensity of children to engage in such unfamiliar topics is featured in the foreword to Kieren Egan's book, *Children's Minds, Talking Rabbits and Clockwork Oranges* (1999), in which Elliott Eisner comments that:

> it is faulty to assume that youngsters do not have the capacity to understand and find interest in ideas and practices that are not already in their midst. It is precisely the capacities of very young children to exercise their imagination that should be sustained rather than diminished in school. (p. xi)

Eisner adds that educational systems often cultivate 'a logocentric conception of mind that diminishes the imagination and romantic side of human nature' (p. xi). Imagination is seen as frivolous and less important because it is associated with fantasy and play and, 'as we all "know", play is the opposite of work ... play and imagination are at best questionable and at worst a distraction from what really matters' (p. xi).

Through the numerous examples of children's work in this book, I aim to illustrate how imagination, creativity, fantasy and play are fundamental components of young children's art and meaning-making. Art involves imagining possibilities. The contents of children's imagination can be realized through the art they make and the meaning that this communicates.

Meaning-making

Without the arts, the history of cultures throughout the world would be very different. Indeed, the arts have always played a significant role in humans' creation and sharing of thoughts and feelings. As Rabiger describes it: 'in every period and in every part of the world, art has supplied a surrogate experience to exercise hearts and minds' (Rabiger, 2008, p. 178).

Our representational practices serve a basic human need – to explore and understand the world in meaningful ways, no matter which medium is used to do so (Danesi, 2007). Chandler (2002, p. 17) described meaning-making as an innately driven characteristic of humans: 'We seem as a species to be driven by a desire to make meanings: above all, we are surely *homo significans* – meaning-makers'.

But, paradoxically, 'by representing the world, we end up changing it, making it virtually impossible for us to distinguish between reality and our representations of it' (Danesi, 2007, p. 122). The famous question by Bertolt Brecht remains: Is art a mirror to society, or a hammer working on it? Does art reflect actuality, or does it change and therefore create it? The answers will vary, but we can say with confidence that representational practices allow us to probe and explore reality and thus 'discover' the elements of reality and the 'hidden principles' that govern human life and the universe (Danesi, 2007, p. 132–133).

Through art, people of all ages make an object of their own contemplation. They use symbols to manipulate images and concepts, which is linked to the creative process of meaning-making. Art allows us to create a symbolic world and to 'shape and reshape, revise and revision' our own 'hidden and subjective' lives (Abbs, 2003, p. 13). Art gives shape to formless ideas. It is a vehicle by which we can express our growing awareness of ourselves and the worlds in which we live. This provides a powerful mechanism for reaching the deepest, richest, most abstract aspects of our existence. The process can engender a sense of freedom, release, fulfilment and wholeness – sometimes to the point of ecstasy – because it connects with deep levels of symbol, meaning and emotion. The arts help us place our objects, our activities and ourselves in a larger existential framework, where we are actually 'touched' through a different way of understanding.

Art making and its narrative description of the here and now (Kellman, 1995), allows children to share the day-to-day details of their lives with others. But beyond the 'here and now', art making also allows children to explore abstract and complex concepts, such as what the future may be like. Because multiple options are available for the future, this topic is an inspiration for creative thought, as it delves into the intangible, the 'what might be'. Kellman notes that art making, coupled with narrative, is a 'means of inventing, a method of thinking, a way of giving life to hopes and dreams' (Kellman, 1995, p. 19). In a similar vein, Rabiger (2008, p. 129) states that, 'to make fiction is to propose reality'.

Art making involves thinking in symbols, which Dewey in his book *Art as Experience* (1934/1988) described as one of the most sophisticated modes of thought. The human child is endowed with ingenuity and symbol-making propensities to go beyond reality as immediate experience. By using the symbolic system of drawing, children manipulate images and concepts, thus joining with others who share a culture, who share the same 'imaginative universe' or 'worlds of possibility' (Dyson, 1993, p. 23). This capacity is at its peak in early childhood.

Early childhood is a time when children's thinking is still imaginative, flexible and linked to fantasy and fiction. Yet, imaginative and fictional qualities are what young children begin to lose as they grow older, and what adults should seek to rediscover. The future-conscious teacher is led to prefer a curriculum that supports these qualities, and encourages thought process that will help children develop concepts that will prepare them for what is likely to happen (Egan, 1999, p. 78). But in addition to exploring *probable* options for the future, pedagogy should also help children explore concepts of *possible* and *preferable* options (Eckersley, 1992, 1999; Slaughter, 1994a).

Future-conscious teachers aim to equip children to become autonomous and active *creators of the future*, through skills such as adaptability, imagination, fantasy, altruism, sensitivity towards others, decision-making, resilience, empathy, an interest in other cultures, and abilities in communication, problem solving and lateral thinking (Wright, 2001). As Egan (1999, p. 78) describes curriculum, it should encourage 'critical thinking rather than knowledge acquisition, problem-solving skills rather than familiarity with past problems, openness to change rather than commitment to a set of ideas and institutions'.

Consequently, meaning-making through drawing is a means for capturing many of these future-oriented values. Through the act of drawing, children's thought, body and emotion unite. Indeed, drawing involves more than simply forming images; it is equated with the capacity to think and to feel (Egan, 1992). Goodman's (1976) reminder is that 'what we know through art is felt in our bones and nerves and muscles as well as grasped by our minds' (in Buckham, 1994, p. 140).

Young children's drawings open a window into their realities and how they shape these. We come to understand the range of a child's thinking and feeling through close observation of the drawing activity itself and the talk that accompanies it. As Cox (2005, p. 124) notes, the constructive process of drawing helps children to 'purposefully bring shape and order to their experience, and in so doing, their drawing activity is actively defining reality, rather than passively reflecting a "given" reality'. The examples of the artworks of children presented in this book demonstrate that, through drawing and talking, children came to not only *know* reality, they *create* it.

Hence, a fundamental component of the work of early childhood educators is to understand what is *meant* by a child's drawing in relation to his/her ideas, actions and feelings. How we may interpret and possibly extend this meaning in our interactions with young children is an important consideration. One approach is through the application of principles derived from the multidisciplinary field of semiotics. Semiotics assigns much weight to creativity and human inventiveness as factors that shape evolution (Danesi, 2007).

To do justice to the topic of creativity, while also providing a context for the value of semiotics in early childhood art education and research, some brief definitions and descriptions will be helpful. These constructs will be revisited several times throughout this book, supported by many examples of children's creations for illustrative purposes. Put simply, semiotics is the study of 'the capacity to create and use signs such as words and symbols for thinking, communicating, reflecting, transmitting and preserving knowledge' (Danesi, 2007, cover note). It provides us with a potentially unifying conceptual framework and a set of methods and concepts for making sense of all kinds of human products, from 'words, symbols, narratives, symphonies, paintings and comic books to scientific theories and mathematical theorems' (Danesi, 2007, pp. 3–4). Semiotics can be applied to the full range of *signifying practices* (Chandler, 2002). These include gesture, body language, facial expressions, eye contact, dress, writing, speech, narratives, the mass media, advertising, drawing, photography, space, cuisine and rituals. In sum, semiotics involves investigating, deciphering, documenting and explaining the *what*, *how* and *why* of signs.

As an approach to communication, semiotics foregrounds how meaning is not passively absorbed, but arises through the active process of sign creation and interpretation. Specific *semiotic modalities* are addressed by such specialists as linguists, art historians, musicologists and anthropologists. But as Chandler (2002, p. 214) points out, 'we must turn to *semioticians* if we wish to study meaning-making and representation *across modalities*' (my italics). Because the act of drawing is multimodal, I aim to make my analytic strategy explicit so that others may apply it either to the examples presented in this book, or to other examples of children's art. Rather than engaging in a debate about various semiotic approaches that might have been applied (e.g., relativism, poststructuralism, traditional structural semiotics), I prefer to adopt a general standpoint that signs are related to their signifieds by social conventions that we learn, and to illustrate some examples of this through the selected presentation of several children's works.

I will focus on how representation, as sign-making, bridges the child's real world 'out there' with his/her inner imagination. Yet I will also foreground how children's drawings represent something according to specific traditions and practices. In other words, representation is not, purely, an open-ended process. It is constrained by social conventions, by communal experiences and by other contextual factors (Danesi, 2007, pp. 122–123). Some of the foundational constructs of semiotics might do with teasing out a little; so let us briefly delve more deeply into signs and how their meaning is communicated in children's drawing texts.

Signs and texts

A sign can be defined simply as 'something that stands for something else in some way' (Danesi, 2007, p. 29). In a broad sense, a sign is anything that communicates meaning. Signs can take many forms. As mentioned above, they can be words, images, sounds, gestures, touch, odours, flavours, acts or objects (Chandler, 2002).

But signs have no intrinsic meaning in and of themselves. They become signs when we invest them with meaning – when we interpret the sign as *standing for* or representing something other than itself. For instance, we interpret a child's meaning when we ask ourselves what is meant by his/her mark on paper, use of a word or gesture, physical action and many other forms of communication. These component parts are what Danesi would refer to as the 'small' signs, which must be seen in relation to the whole artwork and the overall meaning of the child's drawing. In such cases, we are considering the collection of signs as something much 'larger' – as a *text* – and are looking at the text's larger *message* (Danesi, 2007, p. 97).

The child's integrated drawing-narrative-embodied text becomes a single, multimodal communicative act. The constituent parts (the small signs) of speech, image and non-verbal communication (e.g., facial expressions, gesture, body language, expressive vocalizations) are integrated, *holistically*, as a single form. As van Leeuwen (2005, p. 121) metaphorically describes it, multimodal communicative acts such as these, blend 'like instruments in an orchestra'.

Such holistic texts are in stark contrast to texts that are interpreted *linearly* such as numbers in the decimal system, equations and written language. Danesi explains how linear texts are deciphered by means of a sign-by-sign interpretation process. Numbers, for instance, are composed and read in a linear fashion and interpretation is cumulative: 'the value of the entire number (= the text) is gleaned by assessing the values of the individual signs (= the digits in the number)' (Danesi, 2007, p. 98).

By contrast, the component parts of holistic texts, such as drawing and narrative, are not assessed one at a time, but instead, are seen as elements of a whole. Indeed, one element, such as a word, cannot be detached from the accompanying graphic mark or physical gesture without impairing the overall meaning of the text. Susanne Langer referred to meaning creation and communication in art as involving elements, such as lines, shapes, proportions, colours, shadings, perspective and composition, which are 'abstractable and combinatory' (Langer, 1924/1971, pp. 86–89). These elements are as complex as combinations of words, yet they have no vocabulary of units with independent meaning. For instance, there are no items within pictures that might be metaphorically equated to the 'words' of portraiture.

Consequently, compared to 'tight-structured' linear texts, art is a loosely structured and holistic text. This is because the elements of art have so many potential relationships. For instance, the colour pink or a jagged line can have very different meanings according to how they are used within the context of the drawing. Similarly, the placement of an image, such as a bird on the ground versus a bird in the sky, communicates a different meaning. Hence, the range of possibilities of signifying meaning through visual elements, such as colour, or the distance between objects, or the placement of content within a pictorial plane, are virtually infinite.

So we must view children's drawings, combined with their spontaneous running narrative and non-verbal communication, as a single multimodal act. The meaning is constituted by its total effect and understood as a complete whole: as a macro event or a macro sign. As such, the artwork-narrative in its entirety is a *semiotic unit*. Its meaning works at two levels: it is presented not only on the surface level (that which is denoted) but also below the surface (that which is connoted).

Levels of meaning

As a human species, we interpret each other's meaning almost unconsciously, by relating signs to familiar *systems of conventions*. Indeed, we are so used to using the systems of words, pictures, numbers, gestures, touch, sounds and many other signs in our everyday life that we generally don't stop to think about how we do this, how important these sign systems are to human communication, how they have derived or how we have learned them. Humans have invented a number of *sign systems* for representing ideas and experiences, such as language, art, music, maths, physics, dance and history. We use these sign systems to make ideas and experiences a public, shared form of communication that can be understood by others. Indeed, as Eco (1976) states, these systems form the basis for creative and critical thought processes.

Hence, as teachers of young children, our goal is to understand the principles that children use in their representations of the world. Whether this be in relation to mathematics, literacy or the arts, it would be virtually impossible for teachers to communicate the content of education, or to understand the layers of meaning in children's communication, without understanding our shared systems of meaning.

The study of children's meaning and their inherent 'layers of text' is linked to the branch of semiotics called, generally, *hermeneutics*. Danesi (2007) describes the defining methodological features of classical hermeneutics as involving an analysis of:

- a surface (signifier) level consisting of constituent forms (sentences, words, phrases, etc.), and
- a deep (signified) level, which contains its true (sometimes called 'hidden') meanings (pp. 105–106).

The 'smaller' signs, such as words, images (e.g., colours, lines, shapes, textures, composition, etc.) and gestures, are the 'signifiers' in children's visual-narrative texts. They combine in order to communicate some overarching message – or the 'larger signified' – which is the 'something else' for which a physical structure stands (Danesi, 2007, p. 29). So we must 'look behind or beneath the surface' (Chandler, 2002, p. 214) of a child's drawing in order to discover its underlying organization and meaning. This requires noting the child's use of art elements in relation to words, gesticulations, dramatic vocalization, pauses or hesitations, and how art elements are combined with language and movement to carry meaning (i.e., what they 'stand for').

Following on from the work of the visual semiotician Roland Barthes (1957/1973, 1977), layers of meaning are given the terms *denotation* (surface level) and *connotation* (deep level). Barthes (1977) described denotation as the *literal message*, such as the depicted people, places, objects and events, and connotation as the *symbolic message*, such as the broader, abstract concepts, ideas and values being expressed. Abstract concepts, like 'love', 'friendship' and 'justice' are especially high in connotation. Such concepts are understood as culturally shared meanings (Barthes, 1977) and are communicated in visual forms through association. Some examples of connotative associations of *what* the represented people, places, objects and events stand for might include, for instance:

- people's poses (e.g., arms raised heavenwards, which may connote exuberance)
- places (e.g., a playground, which may connote fun and games)
- objects (e.g., a bookcase, which may connote intellectual ideas)
- events (e.g., a running person, which may connote fleeing or freedom).

Hence, connotation is not only about *what* is being communicated but also *how* this is done through the use of aesthetic form, such as the arrangements chosen to visually present the people, places, objects and events. This includes aspects such as:

- techniques (e.g., shading, bold lines, strong contrasts, angle, framing)
- style (e.g., the child's own artistic identity or 'individual stamp' on the artwork).

As a simplified illustration of this, the message of the artwork presented in the opening of this chapter (Figure 1.1) has two layers.

Figure 1.2   Olympic Equestrian Event (girl, 7.9)

At the denotative level, the man standing on Earth, 'planting' a flag in the soil next to Australia (signifier) denotes that he is 'first' or the 'owner' of Earth (signified). At the connotative level, the profile and angle of the spaceship and the astronaut inside (signifier) connotes that the man is taking off from Earth to fly around in space on 'joy rides' (signified).

By way of a further example, some features in the artwork in Figure 1.2, of an Olympic equestrian event (drawn by a girl, 7.9), include judges seated behind dark desks (i.e., the six figures at the back of the stands). The judges stand out from the crowd of smaller, less clearly defined people who fade into the background as 'secondary' figures, compared to the 'primary' figures of the judges. Most prominently, the competitor in the event is large and central – the focus of the content. The art elements of colour, proportion, shading and perspective all function to communicate that the rider is being judged while competing in the Olympics.

Four creative transformations were used by this young artist while improvising her content. Behind the audience is a scoreboard, which indicates that Australia (Aus) is scoring 2001, and New Zealand (New), 991. The artist decided to change the score, so she *deleted* the original scoreboard by blackening it out and *substituted* this by *adding* a new scoreboard below it. Later in the drawing, she *transposed* the grass behind the jump post into water by drawing swirling blue lines – to make the equestrian event more challenging.

As illustrated in Figure 1.2, and relevant to children's meaning-making, our understanding of their communication within the open-ended framework of art requires us to become sensitive to children's *processes of production* and to their *authorial intentions* (Chandler, 2002, p. 210). Such receptiveness surfaces an awareness of *how* things are being represented by children, rather than only *what* is represented. As Eisner (2002) reminds us: 'How something is said is part and parcel of what is said. The message is in the form-content relationship, a relationship that is most vivid in the arts' (www.infed.org/biblio/eisnerarts_and_the_practice_of_education. htm).

Attention to this relationship is key to understanding the holistic meaning of children's artworks. The work is a macro event in which the signs of words, images and actions are unified into one semiotic unit, and the text's meaning is made through its total effect, as a complete whole. Hence, a final component of this chapter will focus on how children's articulation of meaning during the creative act of drawing is multimodal and 'other worldly', and that the structures that children improvise are fluid.

Visual narratives: improvising in 'other-worldly' ways

Golomb (1988) describes children's representational forms as being the outcome of a 'dialogue among the hand, the eye, and the urge to symbolize reality' (p. 234). Indeed, Vygotsky describes drawing as a kind of 'graphic speech' (Dyson, 1982). One cannot, however, over-look the narrative and non-verbal communicative aspects as compelling features of children's meaning-making while drawing. Yet, because of the emphasis on traditional views of narrative (i.e., from a literacy perspective), far more attention within research has been given to oral storying and story writing than to the important role of visual narrative.

When viewed from a semiotic perspective, children's drawings – as macro events or holistic messages – include an expansive range of signs used in highly interactive, fluid and expressive ways. This involves the depiction of content through *graphic* and *body-based action*, while *talking* about aspects of the artwork and/or the processes of its creation through a free-form type of narrative.

This perspective is aligned with a *conception of mind* (Sutton-Smith, 1995) and the prominence of the role of visual narrative in our ways of making sense of the world and of experience. The work of Bruner (1986), Gardner (1983) and Egan (1999) give us a more detailed understanding of how scripts, schemata and stories are deployed in our meaning-making experiences. They emphasize that the function of narrative is a method of thinking, of sharing experience and of assigning meaning. Narrative is as important in the lives of children as it is in the lives of adults.

Children and adults alike use narrative as a means of constructing their interior, psychological worlds (Goodman in Bruner, 1986). The insights and images in a child's world help us to see through the eyes of the child as he/she reflects on life and constructs 'other' worlds (Kellman, 1995). By examining the narrative in children's art as invention, communication and as a method of solving problems, it is possible to come closer to their interior worlds.

The fantasy-filled narratives concocted by young children seek out the rhythms and patterns of the story form. Yet the content and structure of young children's narratives are often different in important ways from that which typically engages adults (Egan, 1988). Children's depictions of imaginary worlds, while dialoguing with the materials (i.e., paper and felt pens), is more akin to play than to story-telling. Their narratives do not necessarily follow the rules or 'universal form' of story-telling, which Egan (1988, p. 3) described as having 'a beginning which sets up an expectation, a middle that complicates it, and an ending that satisfies or resolves it'.

Instead, children's visual narratives encompass processes whereby people, places, objects and events are 'told' through the child's graphic action – mark-making that depicts ideas and feelings in *real time*. It is a spontaneous unfolding of content that moves in and out of loosely structured themes. The themes of children's thinking generally unfold 'radiationally' (Gallas, 1994) rather than sequentially. Indeed, connections within the content are made and re-made as the child describes his/her evolving ideas – in whatever order these may evolve.

This loosely structured type of thinking is associated with the openness of the *configurational signs* (Arnheim, 1969, 1974), such as people and objects, that are used in the medium of drawing. Configurational signs are similar to their natural referents – a child's drawn tree, for instance, resembles what he/she sees in nature. But compared to syntax in language, which is highly rule governed, configurational signs are ever changing. As Arnheim explains, they offer an open invitation to be altered; for children to elaborate upon their forms. Children, for instance, readily add a hat to a drawn figure, depict the person in a different position, or attach whoosh lines to show that the person is running. This is because the non-standard nature of configurational signs encourages the invention of new visual forms.

Consequently, the running narrative that accompanies a child's drawing is, similarly, ever changing and open to alteration. It responsively 'mirrors' the loose structure that stems from the configurational signs that the child spontaneously constructs. The child uses gestures to describe, locate, relocate and 'play' the characters, objects and events. Yet, when 'playing' through drawing, the dialogue generally is not like conversation, such as asking 'would you like to have a cup of tea?'; a type of dialogue which is more common in children's socio-dramatic play, or solitary play with toys. Rather, the playing of characters and events while drawing is more omniscient, descriptive and indexical, such as, 'this is where she stepped on the stones to get to the other side of the river' (this issue will be discussed in more detail in the next chapter).

In addition, because the child's dialogue is intimately linked to his/her graphic action, it is similar in some ways to the dialogue found in film – it is highly succinct. As Rabiger (2008) explains, film dialogue 'must exclude life's verbosity and repetitiousness' (p. 133). He elaborates: 'In real life, little is denoted (said directly) and much connoted (alluded to in a roundabout way). Silences are often the real "action" during which extraordinary currents flow between the speakers' (p. 133). Similarly, character dialogues in children's visual narratives are full of such silences, the meaning of which must be deduced by the young artist's gestures, expressive vocalisms, facial expression and body-based communication. These, accompanied with graphic action, do the 'talking' of the characters.

The loosely structured meaning that is generated is similar to what Egan (1988) described as *causal schemes*, which are more like plots than stories. Causal schemes determine the organization of the narrative, which is similar to how plots develop during children's play. Egan elaborates that such schemes are 'ordered in sequence by causality' as the plot unfolds, which is determined by 'affective connections' (p. 11), such as, 'these events cause these emotions in people which cause them to do these things which cause these results, and so on' (p. 24). One scene follows another, taking their places in the affective pattern, building coherently towards the overall unit.

Egan's view is that causal schemes grow out of the logic of metaphor, and he cites C.S. Lewis's perspective that the real theme of stories is 'like a state or quality' and an 'empathy with characters' through the 'immersion in other worlds' (Lewis, 1982, p. 18). Others have discussed the other-worldly, special frame of mind the child enters when inventing a pictorial reality through art. Golomb (1988), for instance, states that art transforms children's ordinary experiences of the world and allows them to represent it 'on a new and perhaps mythical plane of action and thought' (p. 222).

Young children's other-worldly ideas, as reflected in their visual narratives, demonstrate the intricate link between their affective, imaginative, rational and abstract thinking. Their narratives, coupled with drawing and action, encapsulate into one compact package, ideas, context and emotion. This offers an authentic kind of participation for the child, and a concrete form through which we can observe the workings of the child's imagination and the role of imagery in his/her thinking. Drawing serves as direct documentation of the diverse concepts that children apply to their personal experiences, to more fully grasp their worlds. Most notably, it enables children to imagine new perspectives, new worlds. Drawing is something the child can inhabit or get inside of. Indeed, drawing is something the child *is*.

It is the integration of three modes in consort – graphic, narrative and embodied – that makes visual narrative a powerful source for children's learning, representational thought and creativity. Body and mind intersect as children discover, through exploration and play, the distinctive features of meaning-making that take place within these modes. Table 1.2 provides a description of these modes and their features. Yet, it should be noted that the examples for each feature are illustrative, rather than forming an exhaustive list of possibilities. Throughout this book, several cases of children's work will be used to illustrate these modes and features, and specific chapters will cover these issues in greater depth.

In sum, the graphic, narrative and embodied modes co-exist while children draw. This multimodal, symbiotic relationship increases children's capacity to use many forms of representation. Many authors have discussed how talk, drawing and movement are parallel and mutually transformative processes – they enrich and inform each other (cf. Dyson, 1986, 1990, 2003; Kendrick & McKay, 2004; Kress, 1997; Matthews, 2004; Short, Kauffman, & Kahn, 2000; Thompson, 1995; Wright, 2003a, 2005). Gallas (1994), for instance, demonstrates that the narratives that children create while drawing are paralleled by their oral storying and role-play. This is 'a constructive process of thinking in action' (Cox, 2005, p. 123). As Linqvist describes it, 'children draw pictures and tell a story at the same time; they act a role and create their lines as they go along' (Linqvist, 2001, p. 8).

Table 1.2   Modes and Features of Meaning in Visual Narratives

Modes	Features	Examples
Graphic	Art elements	Marks, lines, shapes, colours, textures, shadings, proportions, composition and perspective
	Symbols	Letters, words or phrases to label characters, places, objects or events, or to title the work; numbers to quantify content or signify sequences; flags, traffic lights, emblems, badges, motifs, logos
	Icons and iconic devices	Speech balloons to 'voice' the characters; whoosh lines to 'move' the objects or figures; dotted lines to show movement trajectories between things
	Spatial relationships	In front/behind, close/distant, above/below, similar, proximal, surrounded, vertical/horizontal axes
Narrative	Non-Fictional	Real, true-life, personal
	Literal	Descriptive, factual, exact, unembellished
	Fictional	Imaginary, unreal, fantastic, illusory
	Metaphoric	Rhetorical, symbolic, allegorical, abstract, which may include: • figures of speech, such as 'heavy music' • rhyming • onomatopoeia (i.e., the use of a word or vocal expression which sounds like the thing or action designated, such as 'frmmmph')
Embodied	Descriptive action	Moving the hand across or outside the page (e.g., to show spatial relationships or movement)
	Expressiveness	Gesticulations, facial expression, body-language, vocalisms (e.g., emphasis through change in pitch, volume or speed of speech) and gestures to accompany onomatopoeia (e.g., flicking fingers to go with the word 'poooooffff')
	Dramatization	Enacting as if being a character or an object (e.g., demonstrating a steering motion to indicate driving a car)

Using play as the vehicle for their explorations, children selectively and frequently move from one mode to another to represent and re-present what they know most effectively. They may choose to draw it, or to tell it, or to show it through their bodies – or to combine these modes. For instance, sometimes the child might talk about an idea and then show this graphically or through physical action; sometimes the child might draw something, and then talk about it or demonstrate its meaning through vocalisms, dramatization or action; sometimes the child might dramatize an idea and then describe this through language or show it through pictorial content; sometimes these processes are concurrent (e.g., the child might draw a squiggly line below a figure, while simultaneously saying 'Aaaahhhh' and gesturing downward, to show that the person is falling).

So, the signs that children make offer the possibility of representing through a multiplicity of means, at one and the same time (Kress, 1997). Children are 'playing with the process of signing' (Cox, 2005, p. 123), and the integrated text of drawing, talking and role playing becomes what Chandler (2002, p. 3) calls an 'assemblage of signs', or what Goodman (1976, 1984) referred to as a form of integrated 'languages'. It is a discourse using the 'mixed-media' of language, image-making and graphic and physical action. Children experiment with the 'language of materials and marks' (Cox, 2005, p. 122) combined with narrative and embodied telling. In the process, they build concepts and become *authors* of an integrated text, using a range of voices of communication.

Summary

Semiotics helps us realize the affordances and constraints of various modes of communication. This helps us avoid the 'routine privileging of one semiotic mode over another', such as the written over the visual, or the verbal over the non-verbal (Chandler, 2002, p. 219). Through visual narratives, children invent worlds in other-worldly ways to create, represent and communicate meaning. These processes are surfaced through the child's imagination while using the open-ended resources offered – a blank page can 'become' anything. The loosely structured use of the configurational signs offered through art, accompanied by narrative, gesture and role play, provide infinite possibilities for symbolic communication. This liberates children to construct and re-construct visual arrangements on the page and to 'speak' through the medium of graphic, narrative and embodied communication. The message of the *macro text* stems from the child's imagination, personal experiences in the world and exposure to a range of things, such as the media, mentors and opportunities.

Art provides a place where negotiation takes place, where new meaning becomes possible and where new worlds can be developed. While drawing, children enter into an interpretive space where they can 'tell themselves about themselves' (Geertz, 1971, p. 26). To be present in that space is to witness the internal worlds that children imagine, investigate and make real through the images of their art.

Indeed, many aspects of the child's discourse can remain invisible unless we witness his/her creation of the text and understand the multifaceted ways that it evolved. Without an understanding of the child's processes, the drawing itself is merely a stagnant artefact – a remnant which may be filed and stored, or alternatively displayed on a refrigerator door of a home or on the walls of a classroom or gallery. Yet rich understandings of the artwork and the creator can arise when we observe the child's various verbal, visual, spatial and bodily-kinaesthetic forms of representation as they unfold in real time, naturalistically. This involves reflecting on the child's creative process of meaning-making: what the content denotes and how this communicates deeper meaning, connotatively.

Children draw to create meaning and to communicate this with others. They demonstrate incredible control of the process of composing through dialoguing with the materials of art. Meaning-making through visual narrative is a highly creative and 'fluid' process, where children become authors using multiple texts, combining graphic, verbal and embodied modes. In consort, these modes increase children's capacity to represent, to mentally manipulate and to organize their thoughts and feelings. Children's meaning can be understood when the following aspects are considered relationally:

- the *content* (i.e., themes, people, places, objects, events), and
- the *form* in which this content is communicated through three modes:

  - *graphic* (i.e., structural arrangements and use of art elements, symbols, icons and iconic devices),
  - *narrative* (i.e., telling the content and the processes of its creation through various forms – non-fictional, literal, fictional or metaphoric), and
  - *embodied* (i.e., descriptive action, expressiveness or dramatization).

However, open-ended, free exploration through creative processes such as problem setting, problem solving, elaboration and transformation can be denied within the culture of classrooms. Instead, precedence in school often is given to 'teaching' the more rule-bound symbol systems of numeracy and literacy. Yet, as argued in this chapter, learning the more loosely structured, holistic discourse of art is a parallel (if not preliminary) form of literacy development. Children learn to arrange elements such as lines, shapes and colours in a visual composition, attending to how the component parts combine, and how the content and form of their meaning function.

Through art, children discover the power of signs and learn to manipulate these as a means towards defining themselves and their connections with the outside world while also creating fantasy worlds.

(Continued)

(Continued)

Future-oriented educators highlight the importance of developing children's fluid thought processes and skills, such as imagination, fantasy, adaptability, empathy and resilience – all of which equip children to be autonomous and active creators. Young children's thinking is still imaginative, flexible and linked to fantasy – qualities that we should seek to retain in children as they grow older.

Reflections

With permission of the child and his/her teacher and parent, photograph or colour photocopy a drawing that has already been made by a child who is between 4 and 8 years of age. Invite the child to tell you about the drawing and take notes of what was said. With permission, video- or tape-record this conversation so that you can revisit this content for deeper understanding.

1. What is the content of the drawing (i.e., what do the signs stand for)?
2. Did separate or combined art elements of the drawing (e.g., line, colour, shape, arrangement of figures) strike you as holding particular significance?
3. What words and/or gestures were used when the child described the artwork?
4. Do you think you may have understood the child's intentions and meanings better if you had been present to witness the child's creation of the drawing? Why?

Bring the child's drawing to class to discuss these questions with your colleagues.

Additional readings

Anning, A., & Ring, K. (2004). *Making sense of children's drawings.* Berkshire: Open University Press.

Gallas, K. (1994). *The languages of learning: How children talk, write, dance, draw and sing their understanding of the world.* New York: Teachers College Press.

Matthews, J. (2004). The art of infancy. In A. Kindler, E. Eisner, & M. Day (Eds.), *Learning in the visual arts: Handbook of research and policy in art education* (pp. 253–298). Canada: University of British Columbia.

Surfacing the Voices of Children:
The Role of the Interlocutor

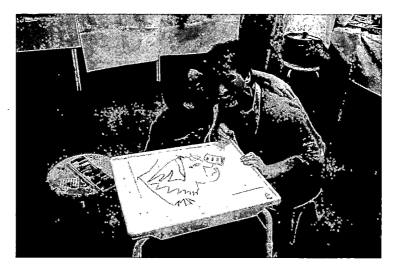

Figure 2.1 Interlocutor with Child

At the completion of this chapter, you should be able to:

1. Understand that childhood is an important phase in human experience, and that art offers a significant play-based opportunity to appreciate the competency of young children,
2. Discuss the child's positioning of self within the drawing (e.g., as subject or spectator), and whether the content is specific to the young artist or meant to stand for 'universal' ideas (i.e., humankind, a rainforest), and
3. Appreciate how children's narratives include ambiguous terms, such as 'this', 'that' or 'there' and how their telling of the drawing is different than storying.

Since the turn of the century, there have been significant shifts in thinking about childhood that have shaped child rearing and educational practice (Brooker, 2001; UNICEF Convention on the Rights of the Child, 1989). Three complementary principles underlie this change in attitude:

- a belief in children's *rights* (including the right to protection from harm, the right to voice opinions and influence decisions in matters relating to their own lives, and the right to be heard and to participate),
- a belief in children's *competence* (their ability to understand, to have perspectives of their own and to make reflective responses), and
- a belief in the importance of *play* in children's lives, including playing through drawing.

Consequently, today childhood is seen as a distinct, intrinsically interesting and important phase in human experience. Children's thinking is not merely 'some embryonic and simple forms of adults' thinking' (Egan, 1999). As Egan elaborates, it 'has distinctive characteristics of its own – some of which are clearly superior to typical adults' thinking' (p. 3) such as 'imaginative skills attached to metaphor and image generation, and to narrative and affective understanding' (p. 88). So, instead of taking a 'deficit' perspective on children's development, judging it as 'immature' against adult standards, researchers are now looking at what children *can do* and how their thoughts and feelings are expressed. As a consequence, there is increasing evidence that young children are more competent than previously supposed, and that early developmental psychologists underestimated children's abilities.

This shift toward more *social constructionist/constructivist* pedagogies and *socio-cultural* perspectives has increased our understanding of how childhood is culturally and historically constructed, rather than being universal and absolute (James & Prout, 1997). Stimulated by the work of Vygotsky (1962, 1967) and Bruner (1996), there is increasing interest in exploring how children's language and play, and artefacts such as drawings, are mediating tools for children to create meaning, within and across cultures (cf. Rogoff, 1990; Wertsch, 1985).

Children's drawings provide a naturalistic way to witness children's creative meaning-making, because the source of the content emerges from the child's own thoughts, feelings and imagination. As Hughes (1996) reminds us, the social purpose of art is 'the creation of mutuality, the passage from feeling into shared meaning' (p. 32).

We can come to understand the child's meaning by attending to the graphic *strategies* that the child uses, the artist's communicative *intentions,* and the *purposes* and *functions* of his/her artwork.

Such an approach is in opposition to the 'deficit model' used in earlier drawing research, which focused on what children *omitted* from their drawings (e.g., eyelashes, the correct number of fingers). In such an approach children's artworks were judged based on developmental yardsticks and stage theories. Such psychologically oriented viewpoints were concerned with the *properties* of the drawing or the child's *behaviour* in isolation of the child's strategies and intentions, or the artwork's purposes and functions. The drawing was viewed simply in relation to a continuum of development – towards a supposedly 'natural' end point of 'realistic' depiction (Cox, 2005). However, as Golomb (1988) points out, when we follow this line of reasoning, we 'misconstrue art making as a process of replication, and judge early art by its failure to establish a one-to-one correspondence between the object's realistic properties and its graphic representation' (p. 226). But, as Golomb elaborates, child art is not concerned with replication but, instead, with 'equivalences of a structural and dynamic kind', and centres on simplicity or economy – children 'use as little as will do' to represent their ideas in a minimalistic way (p. 227).

As will be emphasized throughout this book, we can glean a great deal of insight into a child's meaning-making by 'tuning into' (Trevarthen, 1995) children's unique forms of representing as they interact with paper and felt pens, and observing what the child actually *does* when drawing. Sensitive adult presence is vital to children's creative involvement in art making (Potter & Edens, 2001). By 'being with' the child, we can often sustain and extend his/her interest and involvement. Such interactions have been characterized as 'joint involvement episodes' (Schaffer, 1992). They require empathy with the child's artistic experience and the reciprocity that occurs between the child and the materials (Kolbe, 2000). By attending to the relationships between graphic, narrative and embodied components as the child's ideas and feelings unfold, we are better able to tune into the artwork's purpose and function. For instance, the child's *purpose* may be to represent a bird, yet the child's marks may *function* as a representation of: the flight path of a bird; the rushing wind as it flies; or a range of other meanings.

When we search for both the reason and the meaning of the child's work, our attention centres on how the *features* of the artwork are ascribed aesthetic, intellectual and emotional significance. But the *context* surrounding the drawing may also influence the outcome

(Anning & Ring, 2004; Cox, 2005), and as observers of a child's processes, we become part of this context. Whether we are simply watching and listening, or actively engaging with the child, our presence serves as a form of facilitation. Often simply observing, or perhaps commenting in general (e.g., 'uhum' or 'I see') without further elaboration can be adequate to sustain the experience. At other times, we may be interested in finding out more or obtaining a better understanding of what the child is doing. In this case, we assume the role of *interlocutor*, taking part in a dialogue with the child.

By contrast, when children draw in a private context, his/her narrative is likely to be internalized, perhaps punctuated with some vocalized sound effects, such as 'boooom' to mark a specific event (e.g., an explosion). However, when an interlocutor is present, the narrative becomes externalized. While the interlocutor predominantly assumes the role of audience, in many ways, he/she also serves as a type of playmate with the child, where his/her comments and questions may become a catalyst that enriches the child's play. This may facilitate and protract the experience, and consequently, the play might be more recursive than if the child were playing alone. In some ways, an interlocutor's role is similar to dramatic improvisation. By plunging into a mutual experience, with the child as 'actor' and the adult as 'audience', the interaction becomes relational, interactive, negotiated.

In many ways, the interlocutor role requires a fine balance of reciprocity. Ideally, the child's content should take the lead the majority of the time, with the interlocutor responding rather than directing the play. Sensitive comments usually will be open-ended and responsive, to *surface* the voice of the child rather than *lead* it. Anning and Ring (2004) provide a caution in relation to adult dialoguing with children: 'This involves tuning sensitively into their drawings as they do them; not breathing down their necks and incessantly asking questions such as, "What is it?" but rather entering a dialogue with them' (pp. 119–120). Hence, some open-ended strategies that might elicit a child's elaboration may include:

- *Clarification* ('Can you give me an example of that? What did you mean when you said ...?')
- *Mirroring or reflective probe* ('What I hear you saying is ... Have I understood you correctly?')
- *Nudging probes* ('Really? So what happened then?')
- *Outloud thinking* ('I wonder about ... What do you think?')

Such participation entails reciprocity not only between the *child and the materials* but also between the *child and the interlocutor*. Yet, it is worth noting that children's visual narratives tend to exist in a fragmented form (Wilson & Wilson, 1979). As Labitsi (2007) notes, 'some children develop elaborate settings but do not people them with characters. Some concentrate on drawing actions devoid of any setting; others create characters that never go into action' (p. 185). It is also noteworthy that the child's ideas and depictions may shift in and out of an overall framework, where the complete structure may evolve in bits and pieces. At times the child may be one step ahead of us, explaining the meaning of what has just been drawn while simultaneously drawing a new concept (Wright, 2007a, b). Likewise, the child may return to previous images to elaborate on ideas with graphic or gestural detail, or extend the narrative in relation to these new concepts.

Hence, our sensitive participation with children while drawing requires us to go with the flow of their thinking and depiction. As mentioned earlier, the child's ideas may proceed 'radiationally' (Gallas, 1994) rather than sequentially or hierarchically. There also might be shifts in and out of fantasy and reality. For instance, one boy (6.5) depicted one army man (to represent a full army). Then he said that 'he' (the artist himself) would shoot the house down with his gun. When the interlocutor implied that shooting was not appropriate, the boy shifted out of fantasy role, and changed the narrative from fictional to factual, saying 'that person' (the drawn figure) was 'just playing ... they know better'.

Particularly when a child is engaging in fantasy play while drawing, it is helpful if we can *suspend disbelief* and enter his/her imaginary world. During fantasy-based drawing, a child is immersed in an other-worldly state of mind. We need to recognize the intimate, internalized way the child sustains belief in his/her characters, settings and actions while in this mind frame. But, to complicate matters, some aspects of the drawing may be 'real', whereas other aspects may be imaginary and fictional. As illustrated below, although many components of one boy's (8.0) visual narrative contained elements of fiction, the drawn sun in the top corner of his page functioned simply as a detail in the scenery within the artwork. So when the interlocutor used a nudging probe to enquire about whether the sun (weather) would change in the future (in line with the topic, Futures), he declared the question absurd:

I: Will the sun change or not?

C: No! I don't think it will change into a square or something.

I: What about the weather, will it be the same?

C: Probably.

This example illustrates the delicate process of attending to a child's intentions. As a rule of thumb, it is valuable to avoid doing too much talking. Because children may silently engage with the materials for stretches of time, it can be tempting for adults to want to fill the gaps rather than to allow the communication to unfold on the young artist's terms. Indeed, these silent moments can be highly meaningful. For those who are interested in researching children's meaning-making in more depth, video documentation of the drawing can be helpful for capturing the child's gestures, body language and facial expressions in relation to the unfolding graphic content. It can also be helpful to write synopses of key statements the child made, do rough sketches of the child's marks and their placement on the page and number these to note the sequence in which they were drawn. Transcriptions of parallel streams of graphic, narrative and embodied communication can then be compiled for deeper analyses.

The aim of such research documentation is to make sense of the meanings of the child's words, images and actions. The process is akin to literary studies (Tobin, 2000), where the child's multiple texts can be revisited to deconstruct the composition in relation to its content and form – how the component parts are combined to make up the whole. Such an approach, when used in longitudinal studies, can form the basis for a 'developmental semiotics' analysis of a child's modes of representation over a period of time (cf. Athey, 2007; Gallas, 1994; Kress, 1997; Matthews, 2001, 2004).

Such evidence provides confirmation of children's competence in communicating sophisticated ideas and feelings through the play-oriented, creative and open-ended process of drawing. It also provides powerful illustrations of the significance of art in children's lives, and its importance and relevance within the school curriculum. To understand the content and form of the child's meaning-making, a starting point is to ask ourselves, 'what is being indicated within this representation' and, 'how is this being expressed?' Hence, the next section focuses on children's reference-based communication.

Understanding 'with reference to ... ' thinking

In human communication, when we refer to something, we intentionally direct someone's attention to something. But the words we use when we refer to something can be ambiguous, such as 'that', 'this', 'here', 'there', or sentences such as 'that thing over there'. Such terms are called indexes – they *indicate* something (Pierce, 1931–1958, 2.285).

Stated simply, an *index* is a sign that involves a relation of some kind – it is designed to place referents in relation to one another or to the contexts in which they occur (Danesi, 2007, p. 44). Hence, we need to understand the meaning of the index – what is being indicated – within the context of the communication. Danesi elaborates:

> A perfect example of an indexical sign is the pointing index finger, which we use instinctively from birth to point out and locate things, people, and events. This sign emphasizes, again, the importance of the hands in knowledge making and communication. (p. 45)

In addition to the use of indexical signs, children frequently use *indexical terms* when they draw. For instance, in a child's statement such as, 'this is where the bomb went off', the word 'this' might indicate a number of things. So, to direct our attention to the child's meaning, we must tune into his/her 'with reference to' thinking. The word 'this' might indicate, for instance:

- the *location* of the event on the page,
- the shift of focus to a new *'scene'* in the drawing, or
- the *enactment* of the explosion, such as the child's use of an 'explosive' gesture or an iconic device (e.g., zigzagging lines arching over the drawn sky).

Danesi (2007, p. 45) identified four main types of indexes, which I have summarized below to help orient the meaning of the examples of children's work illustrated in this chapter:

1. *Location* indexes, which involve spatial contexts (e.g., the pointing index finger, and demonstrative words such as *this* or *that*, adverbs like *here* or *there*, and figures such as arrows) which allow 'sign users to indicate their physical location with respect to something (*near, far, here, there*, etc.) or else to indicate the relative location of some referent in spatial terms',
2. *Temporal* indexes, which relate referents to one another in terms of time (e.g., adverbs such as *before, after, now*, and *then* and time units (hours, minutes, etc.)
3. *Identification* indexes, which relate 'the participants involved in a specific, situation or context to one another', such as personal pronouns (*I, you, he, she*, or *they*, or indefinite pronouns such as *the one*, or *the other*), and
4. *Organizational* indexes, which allow us to 'organize, classify, or categorize things in relation to one another or to other things (e.g., the arrangement of books in alphabetical order on library shelves)'.

Indexical signs in children's artworks will be illustrated below through some examples of their use of 'arrows', a 'clock' and a 'thermometer' to indicate concepts of direction, time and temperature. By encountering indexical signs such as these in their daily lives, children learn that a directional signpost indicates that a particular landmark is 'that way', that a clock indicates the 'time of day' and that a high temperature on a thermometer indicates that it is a 'hot day'. Such icons function as indexes in the following ways, where the index (i.e., direction, time, temperature) is connected to its object (i.e., arrow, clock, thermometer) as standing for a concept (i.e., 'that way', 'time of day', 'hot day').

Yet the relationship between the index and object is not based on resemblance. For instance, an arrow pointing to a school refers to the direction of the school, but does not resemble the school; a thermometer refers to temperature, but what does temperature look like? What does time look like? Because these are intangible, relative concepts, our understanding of the index involves an act of judgement. We need to make an inference about what it means.

Sometimes children will elaborate on their meaning, as in an example by a boy (6.6) who drew and described a thermometer:

> At the top of the letterbox, there's a blue thing ... sort of like ... the weather. And it takes the temperature. When it's cold, it puts the number across the line and when it's hot, it puts the number across the [another] line. And it takes the temperature.

At other times, the child's use of an index is not so clear. Hence, the inferences we make will be based on a combination of intuition, our understanding of children and our knowledge of the medium of drawing. This is the case particularly when children represent concepts graphically but not verbally. For instance, the boy's (6.6) drawing shown in the introduction to Chapter 1, which topographically depicted a man landing on Earth, was not described in detail. The artist's placement of the flag close to the outline of the continent of Australia indicates *location* in space and the compass to the right of the flag indicates *directionality*. Yet, when asked about the meaning of the arrows and letters on the compass (N, W, 'A', E), the boy simply shrugged his shoulders. The artwork is entitled, *The Off*, which could stand for either 'the Earth' or the 'lift off' of the space ship; both meanings are simultaneously plausible.

The example in Figure 2.2 is full of indexical signs. It depicts a time machine (centre of page, with 'time' written in the monitor), which is inside a room – the door on the right leads outside. The drawing

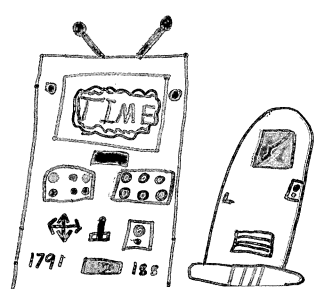

Figure 2.2   Time Machine (boy, 8.5)

includes arrows (bottom left-hand section of the time machine) and a range of other icons. The boy (8.5) communicated concepts of time, directionality and embodied understanding. In the excerpt of the transcription, square-bracketed interpretations have been inserted to clarify the meaning of ambiguous indexical terms (e.g., this, there, them, they, that, it). These interpretations were gleaned from numerous reviews of the video footage and written transcription. Graphic content is italicized and gestural content is round-bracketed and italicized.

C: So, the arrows are for forwards and backwards and sideways.

I: Tell me how the time machine works.

C: Ah ... This [time] is one hundred and twenty-seven times the year 2045. *Adds two sets of numbers: 1791 and 188.* You go back [in time], backwards, not forwards. Mostly everything is changed [since the past]. So if you want to see where they are, the people back in time, you can go. If there was a treasure that they forgot all about, then afterwards they could go back into that year and collect it. [I could] go back in time and collect the things I have dropped or something. *Adds two aerials on top of the time machine.*

I: What are those?

C: Aerials *(claps hands softly together to enact the electro-magnetic waves between them). Adds a joy stick near the numbers, and a speaker to the right of it. To the right of the time machine, he draws an arched door, with an L-shaped handle on the left, a window at the top, a circulation vent below and a landing at the bottom.*

I: Would you like to tell me about those other dials there [above the speaker, joystick and arrows on the time machine]?

C: They use them *(points to two buttons on the time machine panel)* to speak to them *(points to the door to the right of the time machine)* and tell them something maybe. That [door] is where the person that's going into it [the time machine] walks in. They walk in and then it [the date indicator] tells them what time, and then they go off in time.

I: So if I wanted to travel in time, then I would tell the person, and then I would walk into that room and shut the door, and then they could …

C: Press the button [to go].

I: When I wanted to come back, what would I do?

C: Umm, you speak into the speaker. I'll just draw that. *Adds a small speaker on the right-hand side of the door to represent the recipient of the spoken message.*

As illustrated in the bracketed words, we pick up children's meaning by noting the inferences in their words, configurational signs and gestures. Inferring *what* is being communicated, and *how*, can be challenging, since young children's referents (e.g., characters, places, objects and events) can shift regularly within one drawing-telling. For instance, if a child says, 'and now she is going to throw the ball over there', the meaning of 'she' and 'there' must be understood in relation to the region on the page. If we know who 'she' is ahead of time, we are in a better position to interpret the 'there' – or the 'that way', 'up here', 'on that' or whatever directional or relational aspect is being indicated.

Such orientation-based indexes were demonstrated in the example of a boy's (8.2) drawing of a surveillance system. A detail of the full drawing-telling is presented to focus on one segment of the complete work (Figure 2.3). The composition contains several interfaced TV monitors, some of which can be seen in this detail. The boy is describing a complex unlocking system that activates these monitors. Reading from right to left, he describes:

– a keyhole,
– a 'computer prompt' to enter a secret code,
– a keypad on which one enters this code,
– a sign (an arrow pointing to the safe), and
– a safe (which requires another code to unlock it) with a key inside, to activate the system.

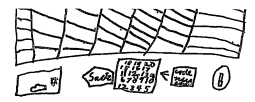

Figure 2.3   Surveillance System [detail] (boy, 8.2)

Well, that [key hole, far right] … you have to get the key [far left], and then it says [prompts] 'the code numbers'. *Writes 'code numbers' inside the square left of the key hole, and adds an arrow pointing to the left to indicate 'move to the keypad'.*

You gotta select a code though. And you gotta select the numbers in. *Adds numbers inside the keypad.*

And then … you've gotta come over here. Writes 'save' [safe] enclosed in a left-pointing arrow.

And then you gotta like … like, that's to like sorta get the TV powered on. Those [TV monitors above] gotta open up first.

So then you gotta select the numbers in [the keypad] … and then you gotta come over here and use the safe. *Draws a combination dial and a key inside the safe.* And you gotta um, turn the thing [dial] and how the numbers go in … the codes of the number … like, another code number.

And then you get the key, and turn that [key-hole on right hand side], and then these [TV monitors] will go on. I mean, they'll open up.

As illustrated by this example and in *The Off*, the interlocutor's role in understanding the child's meaning can be a complex task. It requires attending to the child's use of indexical terms and indexical signs within his/her artwork. It also involves understanding how the child is positioning him/herself in relation to the artwork. For instance, at times the people, places, objects and events may be personal to the child (e.g., me, our house, Dad's car, family picnic); at other times the meaning is more universal (e.g., people, spaceships, time travel). Because the child may shift between personal and universal, it is helpful to tune into the child's agency within the artwork.

Agency and polyvocality

A child's participation in the visual narrative plays a part in the 'constitution of the subject' (Chandler, 2002, p. 91) – in other words, the child's creation of the content of the work is closely linked to his/her world view and personal identity. This process is similar to how one identifies with characters in a film or novel – we put ourselves 'in their shoes' and see the world from their perspectives. As Pahl and Rowsell (2005) assert, we tell stories not only about who we are, but also who we would like to be. She elaborates that, within narratives, identity can be glimpsed, transformed or mediated as children present a retold version of themselves. Indeed, a re-told story 'can be one in which a person "finds themselves" and becomes transformed' (Pahl and Rowsell, 2005, p. 42).

Yet, because of the fluid nature of the child's authorship of the content, at times it is difficult to distinguish between the *child-as-creator* and the *child-as-created* or between the *child-as-subject* and the *child-as-spectator* (Wright, 2007b). This is because, as author-artist, the child simultaneously participates *inside* and *outside* the creative experience. This integrated insider-outsider positioning of self is reflected in the child's accompanying narrative, which often shifts between two foci:

- enacting the character and/or event through *first-person* narration (as if being *inside* the experience), or alternatively
- describing the character and/or event through *third-person* narration, similar to that of a documentary (as if being *outside* the experience).

This shifting between being *depicted* (embodying or enacting the character) and being the *depicter* (impartially drawing-telling the character) was revealed within a single sentence in the following example of a girl's (5.7) description of a police officer's capturing of a criminal (Figure 2.4). The artist said: '*I'm* gonna … and *she's* gonna grab the gun off him'.

The italicized words in this statement emphasize how the artist was simultaneously enacting (i.e., identifying with the police officer, sort of like role playing) and 'graphic-ing' (i.e., drawing the event of the police officer's work). The drawing of the handcuff touching the bad guy's gun became the enactment of the event on paper, similar to dramatic play. Then, as if recognizing the dilemma with being both depicter and depicted, the girl reverted from *subject* to *spectator* by shifting from identifying with the police officer role (*I'm* gonna) to telling the event as an impersonal third-person narration (*she's* gonna).

As in dramatic play, children are conscious of how visual narratives allow them to *suspend disbelief* – they accept the premise that their

Figure 2.4   Police Officer Catching Baddies (girl, 5.7)

work functions as fiction and are comfortable playing with this illusion. Indicators that the child is simultaneously depicting him/herself as the creator and subject are through actions, such as touching the figure in the drawing to show personal identification. For instance, when one 9-year-old girl was asked how old she might be in her drawing of the future, she replied 'About 54', and then touched the figure that represented her. Similarly, two girls (8.0 and 8.2) drew people picking and holding flowers, and one said, 'I've picked up the flower and I'm smelling it'. The themes of these works centred on other sensory aspects, such as living in the country, because it 'is quiet and peaceful'.

When sensory connections such as smell, touch or sound are described as if the artist is experiencing these, there appears to be a type of personal embodiment with the drawing. This is illustrated by a 5-year-old girl in Figure 2.5, who described needing to wear shoes so that she wouldn't cut her feet when walking on the sharp rocks.

> They're the rocks ... But there might be prickles ... If I wasn't wearing shoes I would probably step on the sharp rocks and cut myself. There's the sharp rocks (*points to the rocks*).

Figure 2.5   Walking on Sharp Rocks (girl, 5.0)

Another girl's (5.7) sensory connections within her visual narrative depicts herself giving birth to a baby (whose head is peeping out from the top of her tummy) (Figure 2.6). Yet the artist seems to have either a misunderstanding of the natural birthing process or else an awareness of the caesarean process and anaesthetics.

> [This is] me lying down having a baby. See, there is his head. I am having a sleep ... while the baby's coming out.

Having identified herself as the patient, the artist seems to embody what it would be like to lie on the operating table, and describes this in relation to the need for even-length table legs:

> I want it [the component parts of the table] to be all the right size so it won't be wobbly.

Other sensory-based issues are expressed when the artist draws the ceiling, windows and floor of the operating room. She discovers that sections of the ceiling which have not been completely coloured-in look like holes, which she creatively transforms into being lights in the ceiling.

Figure 2.6   Having a Baby (girl, 5.7)

> [I'll] colour up here so it [the ceiling] looks good. Hey look what I did?
> Holes in the picture, so they could be lights! Colour, colour, colour
> *[verbalised action of colouring in]*.

Finally, a sensory connection is made between the feel of the ink on
the page, which the artist associates with wet paint on the ceiling. As
if she were the painter of the hospital ceiling, the artist's embodied
experience becomes turned into saying that she would leave a sign –
either at 'the hospital' or attached to the drawing itself – to notify
others to be cautious of the wetness: 'It feels like paint this, wet paint.
I will put a sign saying "wet paint" on this'.

This girl, like other children, felt at liberty to alter the framework of
her depiction (e.g., turning the 'holes' into 'lights'). Such alterations
may include changing the roles of characters or modifying events to
suit the artist's purpose. For instance, children can take on the roles of
one or all of the characters in their drawing-telling, and alter these at
will in relation to the evolving plot of their artwork (Wright, 2007b).

Often this shifting of role is done subtly, almost unconsciously, as in
the example above (i.e., *'I'm* gonna – *She's* gonna'). At other times,
shifts in identification are conscious and directly stated, as in the case

of one 6-year-old boy who drew a musician performing on stage. Originally the boy said that the drawn figure was his father, but as the plot and the boy's identification with the character developed, the pop-culture heroism of the content seemed to overtake his impersonal, third-person frame of mind and he announced: 'I want this to be me'.

Such moving in-and-out-of identifying with particular characters is similar to *polyvocality*. In *polyvocality*, commentary shifts from person to person within a text, similar to that of a film (Chandler, 2002, p. 189). Yet, in a child's visual narrative, there is only one person authoring the text. Because of this, the child may choose to 'be' all of the characters and can imagine participating in all of the events. The child's act of drawing the figures gives each character a form, a type of being. In this sense, each of the characters and events assumes some element of the author's fictional self, similar to how a child, during play, shifts in and out of various roles (e.g., 'I'll be the mother ... Ok, now I'm the baby').

Hence, as young artists depict and describe the figures and events within their texts, they use multiple voices and take on many roles. Each character is *enacted* (spoken for) and *narrated* (spoken about) as the artist moves between characters and events. At times, the same character may play more than one event, and these may be depicted in different spaces on the page. As illustrated in the opening to Chapter 1, the figure in *The Off* first planted the flag in the soil of Australia and then he went for a trip in his spaceship. Similar to dramatic play, the child shifted the role of the character to enact two separate events ('I'm the first man on earth ... OK, now I'm going for a joy ride to look at things in outer space').

In summary, polyvocality offers multiple tellings and multiple readings of the characters and events within a child's artwork. A central aspect of understanding a child's meaning requires an awareness of the agency of the narrator, and the fluid functions of the content within his/her artwork. As mentioned above, some enactments can be either personal, as if the artist is being the character *doing* the event, or more impersonal, as if *talking about* the character or event. The simultaneous sense of child-as-creator and child-as-created evolves as the voices of each of the characters and events come 'alive'. This requires an adult's ability to suspend disbelief and to go with the flow of the child's representations of thoughts and feelings.

Yet, as will be discussed in the next section, at times the characters, objects or events within an artwork may not be closely aligned with the artist's personal or fictional self. Instead, the child's depictions may be meant to represent a larger, more prototypical idea, such as 'mankind' (rather than 'a person') or 'everywhere' (rather than 'here'). Such messages are more universal or ideological, rather than personal – they are prototypical.

Signs as prototypes

The identity or role of a particular drawn figure or object, or the enactment of a particular event, may be assumed by the child to be understood and apparent to an adult. Yet ambiguity can be caused by the fact that the child's use of a sign has the potential to stand for either a *specific* object (e.g., a police officer's handcuffs) and event (e.g., the act of handcuffing a person), or alternatively, a *generic* concept (e.g., law enforcement).

When a generic or universal concept is depicted, the child's sign is meant to be read as a *prototype* – a universal representation that stands for a broad category. For instance, a drawn figure may stand for a generic 'human' rather than a particular person, such as 'Mummy' or 'Me' (Wright, 2003a). Similarly, a child's schematic drawing of objects, such as a house, animal or car, can stand for a prototypical idea rather than specific versions of these concepts. For instance, a house can universally represent an 'abode', a 'dwelling', a 'residence', or an 'address', not necessarily a particular home.

As an example, one boy (6.4) drew stick figures of Olympic athletes running around a track, but only one 'green person' was used to represent Australia, and one 'red person' stood for Canada. These representative athletes stood for the many competitors from various countries participating in the Olympics. Similar prototypes of Olympic athletes were illustrated by another boy (8.0), and his comment indicated that matters such as gender, or the type of Olympic event drawn, were irrelevant – the figures were representative Olympians, and the prototypic event was the depiction of first-, second- and third-place winners receiving bronze, silver and gold medals:

I: Is this, ah runner, anyone you know?

C: No, just a person.

I: Man or woman?

C: I don't have a clue [nor do I care]!

I: Could be either.

Recognizing that characters, objects and events may be prototypical, rather than specific, assists the interlocutor to listen for the child's

Figure 2.7   Fairy and Secret Garden (girl, 5.0)

meaning in relation to his/her purpose. In the process of listening, it is helpful to allow the child's content to emerge as naturally as possible, rather than to impose a personal, adult perspective (e.g., assuming that the boy may be depicting a particular athlete that he might admire).

An interlocutor's misunderstanding of an artist's prototypical figure is illustrated in Figure 2.7, where a 5-year-old girl's schema for a 'person' was meant to function differently from the norm. The figure has extremely long hair, a long central line to stand for the 'core' of the body, and billowing, wing-like shapes to represent the dress. These features assist in communicating that this is not an 'ordinary' person but, as the telling unfolds, it is a fairy.

Yet, the interlocutor began questioning the young girl as if the figure was meant to represent the artist herself – 'is it you?'; 'you're a bride!' The girl did not correct these assumptions, but instead nonverbally complied by nodding in agreement and subsequently, in her telling of the event, referred to the figure as 'me'. However, graphically she continued to develop the content to suit her own purposes, and the figure was meant to stand for a fairy in her secret garden. A segment of the transcript below illustrates the subtle way in which the young artist asserted the agency of the figure and its function.

I: Wow, that's beautiful. Tell me about this person. Is it you when you grow up?

C: (*Nods head yes.*)

I: Tell me about what is on there [on the person].

C: This is my [her] head. These are my two eyes and this is my mouth.

I: What is the pink?

C: Um, the dress.

I: It's a beautiful dress. Where are you going in that beautiful dress?

C: A wedding [or something]?

I: Oh, you're a bride! Are you going to get married in that beautiful dress?

C: (*Nods*) *but continues to draw the fairy.*

I: What's this bit [the tall narrow triangular shape on the right-hand side of the page]?

C: The house, and that's the secret garden ... That's grass [below the trees] ... At the bottom [of the garden] is rocks and um, they're the trees, like we have on the secret garden. That's the house.

I: And why is it a secret?

C: Umm, because it's a fairy house.

I: What's it going to be like inside this house?

C: Umm, beautiful things.

The artist, ultimately, clarified that the figure was a fairy (not herself). There were many aspects of the drawing-telling where the graphic content, such as the fairy's house and secret garden, was intended to 'speak for itself'. The artist silently layered the imagery to reveal the fairy's billowing wings and the organic other-worldliness of the house and garden. Her artwork was intended to function as fantasy, and the preschool girl seemed to assume the adult could imagine for herself the details of the garden and what it would be like inside the house – further elaboration appeared to be unnecessary, redundant. Implicitly, the girl expected the interlocutor to suspend disbelief along with her and to fill in the spaces left silent.

Her preschool mind frame embraced the open-ended opportunity for fantasy-based meaning. This is reflected in her economic use of language in response to the question 'what's it *going to be like* inside

Figure 2.8   Driver Training (boy, 5.9)

this house'? When she simply replied, 'beautiful things', the meaning could infer a number of ideas: that there would be beautiful *objects* and resources inside, such as nice furniture, good food, beautiful paintings on the walls and peaceful music. Alternatively, it could be interpreted to mean that beautiful *events* would occur there, such as dining and dancing with friends. The fluid nature of this child's imaginative thinking, like that of many other children's, contained play-like qualities, where anything is possible, anything can be. As interlocutors, it is best if we can go with the flow of young children's mind frames, allowing for their creation of such other-worldly ideas by suspending disbelief in order to 'hear' the children's 'voices'.

Hence, the content and form of children's representations are open to multiple roles, multiple tellings, multiple interpretations and multiple functions. The events, objects and characters that may function originally in one way may be altered to function in another way later in the drawing-telling, depending upon the child's purpose. An example of this is illustrated by a boy (5.9), who originally describes himself as getting some bags out of the boot (trunk) of his car after coming home from shopping (Figure 2.8).

Later, after explaining that he will work as a driver-trainer (in the future) and have his own company car with a Driver Training sign on the top, he changed the function of the boot from containing groceries to containing a battery (which he needed to turn on to light up the sign after dark).

> I'm just getting the spare battery out of the boot. And, ah, the cardboard [sign] has a light on it so you can see it at dark night too. *Adds 'radiating' lines from the headlights, taillights and the sign on top of the car.*

The boot of the car had many purposes, and the shifting of meaning within the context of the car's boot was akin to the changing of a scene in a film. First he does *grocery shopping*, then the scene shifts to him doing *driver training*. This is similar to the shift in scenes in *The Off*, from planting a flag to taking a trip in a space ship. These altered roles and patterns of events all contribute to the child's unfolding of what Egan (1988) referred to as 'causal schemes'. Such schemes when communicated through children's visual narratives are structured around either personal experiences, or based on generic, universal concepts – or a combination of both.

Turning experience or universal themes into narratives

In relation to the structure of storytelling, Metz (1974) observed that 'a narrative has a beginning and an ending, a fact that simultaneously distinguishes it from the rest of the world' (p. 17). In other words, life is not as clear-cut as may be depicted in a story. Chandler (2002) elaborates on the matter of real life events, and how they are integrated rather than separate episodes: 'There are no "events" in the world. Reality cannot be reduced objectively to discrete temporal units; what counts as an "event" is determined by one's purposes. It is narrative form which creates events' (p. 90).

This is why the term 'visual narrative' rather than *storying* has been used to describe children's processes of generating themes or plots while drawing. These narratives are loosely structured and contain a range of evolving ideas. The themes that are depicted and enacted are like fleeting moments. They unfold within a free-form composition. In many ways, a child's visual narrative is similar to a film – it moves in and out of an overall plot scheme, but generally does not conform to the conventions of having a clear-cut beginning, middle and end. Instead, it is similar to fantasy-based play on paper.

Yet, the themes of children's works also reflect cultural models. They seem to be inspired by a blend of personal events, popular media (often fiction) and world events (non-fiction). For instance, one girl's (7.8) narrative, which is described in more detail in Chapter 3, was influenced by knowledge obtained from watching television:

C: I'm drawing the moon and, I think in the future, there might be some people living on the moon.

I: Oh right. Why do you think people might go and live on the moon?

C: Um, on TV I've seen some programmes about ... in the future they think there might be people living on the moon. So I thought I might

> draw that. It's a picture about what I think is going to happen in the future. People might be interested in living on ... up in space. Like, not just on the moon, but going to all kinds of planets, like Mars, some planets that aren't too cold.
>
> I: Right ... so other places, mmm. Why might they be interested in living in space?
>
> C: Well, maybe, because it's a totally different world, and they might think it's better than living on Earth.

The artist described her understanding of living on other planets in a prototypical way, referring to the figures in her artwork as 'people', in a *universal* sense, who are travelling to different planets. Yet she takes on the idea, projecting a personal perspective of what things might be like living in outer space: 'totally different, better'. Her narrative was like a third-person documentary (e.g. 'people might be interested in ...'; 'they might think ...'). This is in stark contrast to the previously described, *personalized* narrative of the 'I'm/She's gonna grab the gun off him' event, which was a depiction of a particular action taking place in real time.

Nonetheless, whether the children's works are documentary-like or real-time depictions, their running narratives are different to a 'story' that is told after the drawing-telling event. This difference is illustrated in some examples in which children made up stories *after* they had 'told' their characters, objects and events through graphic action.[1] The examples below are either mere descriptions of the graphic content, or a truncated version of themes within their works, such as:

> This is a garden. There is a apple tree. There is a swing. All the things in my garden that I drawed ... One house, and one apple tree, one flower and one swing and one ...
>
> We went skiing ... I dodged trees. I jumped off the hills.

Such examples follow the conventional story format, which generally includes a temporal sequence of events, with a beginning, middle and an end. This is most clear in the following selected examples:

---

[1] It should be noted that in the original design of the study, the interlocutor asked the children if there was a story that went with their artwork, in case some children were not very vocal during the interaction. When it was discovered that most children described mini, episodic narratives throughout the interaction, to tell a story at the end was redundant and imposed a linear form upon the narrative. Consequently, the request for children to tell a story was quickly abandoned, but the examples of stories that emerged provide rich contrasts for illustrative purposes between 'telling' a plot and creating a 'story'.

The camel was walking one day, along the beach. But then he saw a big wavy beach and he saw a big fish, and he thought he might like to eat the fish. And he decided to walk in it [the sea], but he couldn't, and he saw some coconuts, so he decided to get that down, and the end. OK, that's it, that's all my drawing.

When I went to work one day, when grown up, I went to Tanby Seafoods. It was nice down there, and there was seagulls. And I had some things to work on. In the afternoon, I would do some work, and then I would go home.

One day, a man went out to get some bread from the service station. And he had to stop at the traffic lights because they make the man stop. And then, when he came back, he had to stop again because it was still red. And then he went back home.

People [audience] went into the stadium. And Angela and Lucy [performers] sing and dance and lots of things else. And suddenly her friends said, 'come on', and then she bowed and then she went off. I don't know anything else.

Although a common literacy-centric practice in schools is to ask children to tell a story to accompany their completed artworks, the *content* of such stories only vaguely resembles the artwork. After-the-event stories are a pale imitation of the vitality of the child's running commentary that is so central to a visual narrative. A re-told version cannot capture the *form* in which the drawing was composed. It is isolated from the child's real-time graphic-ing, which is so characteristic of children's play. It is separated from the 'soul' of the composition, such as the child's *in situ* facial expressions, expressive vocalizations, dramatizations, gestures to illustrate enactment and personal engagement with the creative act of meaning-making.

Indeed, a child's visual narrative is an integrated verbal-graphic-embodied message. It is a multimodal text that can never be repeated in exactly the same way again. So, for many children, storying 'after the fact' seems to be superfluous – it is not the 'real thing'. Children often feel that there is no need to reiterate, in story form, that which had already been 'said' through the body and hand and through running narrative. This perspective is strongly evident in one boy's (5.8) steadfast refusal to provide a story after drawing-telling a picnic theme involving a child and parents. At the conclusion of a 15-minute dialogue, the artist presumably felt that the creative experience had been fulfilled; that the drawing itself was simply a remnant, an artefact, of the total experience:

I: Now, there is a story in your picture, isn't there?... There's a story that goes with your drawing?

C: No.

I: There's not.

Figure 2.9   Family Picnic (boy, 5.8)

C: No.

I: I thought there was.

C: There isn't.

I: Wasn't there a story about this [picnic]?

C: No, just that I love drawing.

I: Not to write it, just to tell it. Can you tell me it?

C: There's no story!

Perhaps the boy felt that to fit his representation within story conventions would do disservice to the message that had already been
communicated – the graphic, verbal and embodied content *was* the
message, and he refused to re-present this in story form. This seems
pertinent when considering the depth of issues that the boy
addressed in his drawing-telling (Figure 2.9). This included topics
associated with aging, differences in appearance between youth and
the elderly, the importance of longevity and the realities of death.
These issues are featured below

Physical appearance and age

C: I'm drawing me [as a father] when I'm really old.

I: Yes, really old, that would be good.

C: When you're really old, there's stripes on you isn't there? *Divides the father's body into sections and fills these in with a variety of colours.*

I: Stripes, is there?

C: There's lumpy bits isn't there?

I: Whereabouts?

C: On ya.

I: On what?

C: On yourself when you're really old. *Adds coloured sections to the mother. Fills in the boy's body with a single colour, without divisions.*

Age, longevity and death

C: Kids are more aren't they?

I: More what?

C: More.

I: What do you mean by more?

C: They're <u>more</u>!

C: What, more people?

C: No. Moooorrre. More. Kids aren't old. They're not old.

I: No. They're young aren't they?

C: Kids are lucky aren't they? They get more live [sic] don't they?

I: What? You reckon when you're old, you don't have much life?

C: You don't, don't ya?

I: So when you're young you have more life? And you're lucky.

C: Yep. I'm lucky aren't I? Because ... and you know what happened to Pop's friend? She was sitting up reading a book and when she was reading it, she died.

I: Dear oh dear ...

C: He woke up and ... she didn't wake up. Finished (*puts the lid back on the pen*).

Although this artist's graphic content – at least on the surface – presented as rather simplistic, the thoughts behind it were abstract and reflective. The characters in his work did not represent one child and his parents, but prototypes in a universal sense – old people and kids – and the message included life and death. Yet, rather than being morbid, the presentation was matter-of-fact and to the point. The concluding statement, 'She didn't wake up. Finished' has a symbolic finality about it: it suggests both the 'ending' of the drawing-telling (including putting the lid back on the pen), and the 'finish' of the woman's life. Yet the overall message of the drawing-telling resonates with a sense of hope – 'Kids are more aren't they? ... Yep. I'm lucky, aren't I?'

Summary

Current beliefs about children's rights to play complement the values associated with providing opportunities for young children to compose using the *mixed-media* of drawing, gesturing and narrating. As learners and researchers with children, we are privileged to witness the verbal-graphic-embodied competence of children as they dialogue with the art materials and with us. We can surface and hear the 'voices' embedded in a child's meaning-making by entering into a playful, open-ended interaction with him/her, to encourage elaboration and clarification and to sustain the experience. This requires the ability to go with the flow of a child's ideas and feelings and to accept that the content and form of the visual narrative may shift frequently as he/she shapes and re-shapes the creative experience.

This may include many shifts between fiction and non-fiction, and between graphic, narrative and embodied modes as the artwork's purposes and functions evolve. Many *indexical words* (e.g., 'this'), *indexical signs* (e.g., a clock) and *indexical gestures* (e.g., pointing or demonstrating) will be used to indicate something within the work. Sometimes the child's *agency* will be personal, as if he/she are inside the experience (voiced in first-person) and sometimes it may be described as if they are outside the experience (voiced in third-person). Yet the narrative generally does not follow the conventions of storying, with a temporal unfolding of a sequence of events. Instead, it is more *free* form, evolving causally in response to the child's unfolding ideas. In addition, the themes of the drawing-telling may be *specific* (e.g., a particular character, place, object or event), or alternatively, *prototypic* (e.g., standing for 'big picture' things).

An understanding of these complex and integrated issues is important for ensuring that visual narratives are valued as an important creative, meaning-making experience of young children. The content and form of children's verbal, graphic and embodied messages are powerful learning and communication experiences. Our attention to the child's *authorial intentions*, and how the features of the drawing-telling *function*, are key components for understanding the child's meaning.

∿ Reflections

1. While following the protocols of teaching and research ethics (e.g., consent), observe and interact with a young child while he/she is drawing. Video-record the experience by setting up the camera so that it captures the child's graphic, narrative and embodied content. It may also be helpful to audio-record the experience because it is not always easy to hear quiet conversations on video recordings. Aim to use open-ended strategies while dialoguing with the child (see the first section of this chapter on the role of the interlocutor).

2. Write a detailed transcription of a *pertinent component* of the visual narrative (i.e., select a 1–3 minute segment that features some aspect that has been discussed in this chapter, such as indexicality, agency, polyvocality, prototypes or other aspects that strike you). Include details of the *content* and *form* of the child's graphic, narrative and embodied representation by following the conventions of:

   • scripting ('C' for child and 'I' for interlocutor),
   • square bracketing interpreted words and indexes,
   • italicizing drawing actions and images, and
   • italicizing and round bracketing embodied communication (e.g., gestures, facial expressions).

3. Bring the child's drawing and your transcription to class to share with your colleagues. In a small group:

   (a) critique the quality of the *child–interlocutor dialogues*, with a particular focus on the amount of 'air space' given to each participant,
   (b) note whether the child's talk, pictorial content or embodied content lead the process, which then was *clarified* by one of the other modes of communication (e.g., the talk being transformed into dramatization),
   (c) look for examples in which the child was enacting the character or event as if from *inside* the experience (through first-person narrative) or describing characters and events as if from *outside* the experience (through third-person narrative),
   (d) note if there were examples of the child's signs standing for *specific* concepts (e.g., Me, Granny's house, Dad's accident) or *generic* concepts and prototypes (e.g., people, an abode, pollution),

(Continued)

(Continued)

(e) share your understanding of the child's meaning in relation to the targeted focus of the component you have transcribed, and

(f) reflect on whether you have a deeper understanding of a child's meaning-making as a result of serving as an interlocutor throughout the experience, compared to simply talking to the child after the work had been completed (as was the case in the Reflections component of Chapter 1).

Additional readings

Cox, S. (2005). Intention and meaning in young children's drawing. *Journal of Art and Design Education, 24*(2), 115–125.

Golomb, C. (2004). *The child's creation of a pictorial world* (2nd ed.). London: Lawrence Erlbaum.

Kolbe, U. (2000). Seeing beyond marks and forms: Appreciating children's visual thinking. In W. Schiller (ed.), *Thinking through the arts* (pp. 48–60). Amsterdam: Harwood Academic Publisher.

Intratextuality in Drawing-Telling

Figure 3.1   Cat, Dog, Mop and Mill (boy, 5.3)

At the completion of this chapter, you should be able to:

1. Describe how the content of a child's visual narrative can involve internal relations within the text, similar to a cartoon strip (i.e., intratextuality),
2. Discuss how the terms 'draw' and 'write' are often used interchangeably by young children, and how they name and label figures and objects or include speech bubbles and whoosh lines in their artworks to clarify their meaning, and
3. Reflect on how the spatial relationships within children's artworks also carry meaning (e.g., in front/behind, close/distant, above/below).

When children draw, they learn how to differentiate the meanings of separate signs and to see connections between them. As discussed in the previous two chapters, children often make a mark, describe it in words and demonstrate their idea through movement or gesture. In the early stages of development, young children's processes of learning the graphic features of drawing (i.e., art elements, icons and symbols) take place in parallel with the processes of learning letters, words and numerical symbols.

Yet, to recap on previous chapters briefly, the *inter-related* way in which children learn these symbol systems can often be overlooked. The child-centred exploration of mark-making begins to lose ground as the cultural expectation for children to develop numeracy and literacy skills starts to take precedence. Numbers and words begin to assume a privileged status, and adults seem to hold their breath for examples of children's 'legitimate' communication through their ability to read and write these particular texts. Along with this there is an assumption that thinking is primarily linguistic, and that 'skill in reading and writing is a precondition for all meaningful learning' (Gross, 1973, p. 202).

However, drawing and the ensuing talk between children or between adults and children supports the evolution of drawing and later writing (Dyson, 1993). Anning and Ring (2004) emphasize the importance of retaining drawing as a significant form of meaning-making, in parallel with other symbol systems, and caution that:

> ... children should not be made to feel that drawing is only a 'tempo-rary' holding form of symbolic representation leading to mastery of the 'higher level' ability to form letters and numbers. The importance of drawings in their own right should be acknowledged and conveyed to children. (p. 118)

As will be illustrated in this chapter, children's competence in the linguistic mode occurs in parallel with and often is *built upon* knowledge and skills acquired through graphic-narrative-embodied communication. This position is supported by Thompson (2002, p. 193) who argues that literacy grows out of non-verbal contexts of play and physical activities, such as the arts. Thompson (p. 194) elaborates that 'rarely acknowledged, the whole language movement's most fundamental tenets rest on the longstanding practice of good art education' and that schools should 'see art education as the model for teaching in all of our disciplines'.

Indeed, art and play are so interconnected in young children's thinking and learning that some preschool children confuse the terms 'draw' and 'write', or use these terms interchangeably, which would suggest that they do not differentiate between the meaning-making potential of these two symbol systems. Dyson (1986) also notes that these two modes are used in parallel in a process of 'symbol weaving' when children begin to 'write' stories. This is also the case when children 'tell' art. The equivalent status of drawing and writing is reflected in the following comments by two preschool aged boys:

> This [the act of drawing] is how I write. Just how big adults draw [write]. You should see the legs I'm going to write [draw].

> I'm going to write [draw] my Dad now.

Another preschool boy, when asked if he had finished his drawing said:

> Ummhmm, here's the words [the drawing]. There you go [you can have the drawing].

Similarly, when preschool children want to write their names or the titles of their works, they may describe the process of writing as drawing, as illustrated in the comments of two girls:

> And I'll write my name on it. I'll draw [write] it up here.

> How do you draw [write the words], 'Not the Future'?

One preschool girl referred to the process of drawing a house as 'building it'.

> I think I'll build [draw] a house.

Such descriptions of their symbolic processes – as they unfolded – give children's acts of meaning a temporal quality. The drawing-telling process is a real-time enactment of an imaginary event on paper. Indeed, children's graphic intentions often are announced in advance, which implies, 'OK, are you watching now? Here I go'. Hence, the act of, say, 'building' the house, became a form of *graphic foretelling* of an event – like a *silent narration*.

During multimodal communication, children effortlessly weave between many forms of symbolizing and fluidly shift between words, images, touch, gesture and onomatopeia. The content of one sign system is mapped onto the expressive plane of another (Siegel, 1995). This is known as *intratextuality*. Intratextuality involves internal relations within texts. For instance, a newspaper photograph may have a caption, and both the visual and written text can be 'read'. Such texts are organized and articulated in terms of one another. Other examples of intratextual genres are narrated television, film documentaries, cartoons and comics with speech and thought bubbles (Chandler, 2002, p. 201).

When children label objects or events, attach speech bubbles to characters or draw whoosh lines near objects to indicate movement, the text is similar to a photograph with a caption, a cartoon comic or an advertisement. Labels, speech bubbles and whoosh lines help to 'anchor' (Barthes, 1977, 38ff) the reading of the child's drawing-telling. Such articulation of texts is similar to how, as adults, we are aided by the use of images attached to equipment installation instructions, which help us decipher how to connect the wires of a home entertainment centre or how to assemble flat-pack furniture.

So what we may choose to regard as discrete texts can, in fact, lack clear-cut boundaries. Children's visual narratives are abundant with examples of intratextuality. Their multi-modal texts become 'anchored' in the various features of art elements, onomatopoeia, expressive vocalisms and dramatization – these unite as children communicate their meaning. The inter-relationships between the 'small signs' of words, images and actions become articulated within the overall visual narrative text to carry meaning.

This chapter begins by illustrating how children's meaning is anchored by their naming and labelling of characters, places, objects and events within their drawings. It also describes how children often use iconic devices, such as speech bubbles and whoosh lines, to 'voice' the characters and 'move' the objects. Finally, it focuses on how spatial relations within the text also carry meaning, such as whether figures are in front or behind other figures, in close proximity or far apart, or on the left versus the right or on the top versus the bottom of the page. All of these features are part of intratextuality.

Naming, labelling, speech bubbles and whoosh lines

Children's inclusion of naming and labelling, and their use of speech bubbles and whoosh lines (called *iconic devices* or *graphic devices*), is dependent on whether these are relevant to their communication. Indeed, the same child may include graphic devices or use naming or labelling in one drawing, but omit these from another drawing, which may be created only moments later. Like all components of drawing, what is included depends upon the child's *intentions* and how the communication is meant to *function*.

Hence, like all examples presented in this book, those that follow cannot be generalized. Rather, the examples are illustrative of the types of communication that may arise and provide background on how and why such forms of expression occur. It is also worth noting that children's use of naming and labelling, in particular, may occur as a result of their emerging engagement with written text. And their use of iconic devices may arise when the child is particularly interested in 'voicing' the figures (through speech bubbles) or in bringing the artwork 'alive', by indicating that objects or figures are 'active' (through whoosh or movement lines). Consequently, a child's inclusion of such content will vary from time to time.

So let us begin with children's examples of how drawn figures and written letters are given equal aesthetic and representational status within the frame of the page. The interplay between images and words is illustrated in the boy's drawing featured at the opening to this chapter (Figure 3.1). The words 'cat' and 'dog' are written beside the two larger animals. The dog and cat (in profile, with their babies) are differentiated from the upright human figures (mother and child). The theme of young and old is also shown by the inclusion of two side-by-side flowers – one large, one small – and the size differences between the paired human and animal figures. This *pairing* of content – young/old and word/image – establishes a sense of integration, a sort of going-together association. The boy said, 'And I can write cat and dog and mop and mill. I can write any kind of word. I can't write every word, just some words'.

Similar features are shown in another preschool boy's (5.4) work, which includes representations of himself, his parents and his dog (Figure 3.2). The lettering for his name (Liam) is as prominent as the human and animal. The importance of getting the written symbols right is emphasized in his comment:

> I want to write my name and this here. I'm writing an 'A' first, and then a 'I L'. Oh, I've done the wrong thing. L I A A ... there [that's the way it should be].

Older (5–6-year-old) children, who had greater mastery of written text, featured their names using large lettering, multiple colours and decorative features, placing these in focal positions on the page. In such cases, the aesthetic qualities of the lettering gave the words prominence, and implicitly, equivalent status in relation to the graphic

Figure 3.2   Me, Parents and Dog (boy, 5.4)

Figure 3.3   Rainforest, Cloud and Bird (girl, 6.3)

content. One example of this is illustrated in Figure 3.3, where there is
a sense of *unity* and balance between the 'M' in Megan's (6.3) name
and the shape and position of the cloud above the 'framed' rainforest

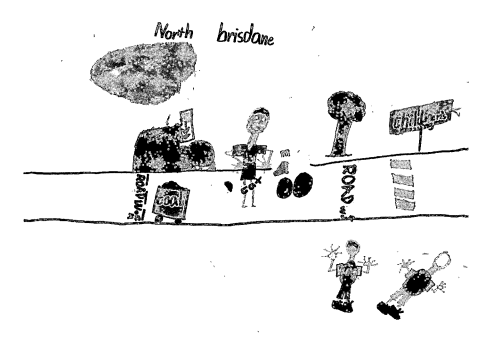

Figure 3.4   North Brisbane Roadworks (boy, 5.7)

below. This creates a complementary aesthetic relationship between the shape of the letter M (symbol) and the angular but rounded cloud (configurational sign). Theo van Leeuwen (2005, p. 13) uses the term *rhyme* to describe two elements, that although separate, have a quality or feature in common, such as shape or roundedness.

Two particularly interesting examples of children's labelled objects are introduced below and will be revisited in more detail in Chapters 4 and 5. The first (boy, 5.7) (Figure 3.4) includes *labels* for the bobcat ('cat') and the coal carriage ('coal'). *Signs* were used beside the road ('children's crossing') and on the road itself ('roadworks'). Two children (bottom right) are waiting to cross the road at the zebra crossing, which is located between them and the 'children's crossing' sign. The artist also used letters to serve another function – to *title* his work 'North brisdane' (North Brisbane roadworks).

A most striking example (Figure 3.5) illustrates that the labels used in the boy's (5.2) drawing were aligned with his embodiment of concepts. Reuban asked the interlocutor to write his name beside the figure (a depiction of himself walking up the stairs after leaving the machine in the shed). He also asked her to write the word 'backhoe' (a digger) beside the machine. But the word 'backhoe' functioned as more than just a *label* for the object. It was meant to describe the

Figure 3.5   Reuban Backhoeing (boy, 5.2)

enactment of the event on the page (i.e., 'doing backhoeing'). As reflected in a segment of the dialogue, Reuban is annoyed with the interlocutor's inability to understand that the word 'backhoe' was meant to function as a verb, not a noun. His vocalism (Danesi, 2007, p. 43) included *increased loudness*; an indication of frustration with his inability to communicate the intended grammatical functions of his labels.

C: Put my name there [far right, beside the stairs 'he' is climbing].

I: Well, that's your name, but what is the picture going to be called?

C: Well I'm *telling* you what I mean. I want to put the name of what I am *doing* ... of what the things are. Now put 'backhoe' just here.

Reuban had an 'ah ha' moment when he looked at the two labels and saw the repetition of letters in the word **ba**ckhoe and in his name Reu**ban**. 'Huh! Backhoe's got one of the bits of my name in it [the letters 'ba'].

   These examples illustrate the significance of visual narratives in children's construction of concepts about themselves and their worlds. These preschool aged children demonstrated an awareness of issues such as:

- living species (e.g., parent/baby 'pairings' of humans, animals and plants),
- physical positioning (e.g., the legs of a figure walking up stairs),
- machine parts and their functions (e.g., the details on the backhoe),
- spatial relations (e.g., cloud and ground),
- signage (e.g., 'children's crossing', 'roadworks'),
- labels ('cat', 'dog', 'coal', 'Reuban'),
- titles of drawings ('North Brisbane'), and
- syntax – learning how verbs and nouns function.

The argument I am making here is that drawing plays an important role in *assisting* children's emergent literacy. However, the act of drawing does not function simply to support other forms of learning. It provides an avenue for children to illustrate their current and evolving competence. What I am emphasizing is that drawing is highly significant as an aesthetic, creative, meaning-making medium in its own right. Contrary to 'folk' belief that drawing should take a subservient role to that of 'literacy' and the teaching of what children don't yet know, I am arguing that drawing is a fundamental form of making meaning which surfaces what children already know, and their further discoveries and learning made during the process of drawing.

As discussed in Chapter 1, drawing is a discourse through an integrated visual-graphic-embodied 'mixed media'. It allows children to 'say' that which cannot be said when only words are used. But most importantly, the words that children use while drawing have soul. As Egan (1999, p. 19) writes, 'the living word' and the 'oral culture' of young children are not like the distanced and cooled word of the written text or the type of learning that often takes place in traditional, literacy-oriented school curricula.

Hence, rather than diminishing the role of drawing as a lesser form of symbol making, it should take a prominent place within the school curriculum. Drawing (and other arts domains) should be the *core* of early childhood education, rather than a second cousin to what is traditionally deemed to be the 'real work' of school – *teaching* the 'school content' of the 3Rs. I aim to illustrate that visual narratives are a fundamental medium for surfacing the meaning-making and creative competence of young children, which I believe positively enhances their disposition to learn.

Intratextuality is a 'natural' and 'logical' way for children to express ideas and feelings. Words, letters, labels, titles and graphic devices help 'anchor' the children's meaning by supporting and enhancing the text's overall meaning. Children use written letters to personalize their artwork, such as writing their names on their work

Figure 3.6   Multiple Drawings (girl, 8.2)

or labelling the content within their drawings. Likewise, they use speech bubbles to give characters 'spoken language' and radiating or wavy lines to 'move' objects. Several examples of these graphic devices are show in Figure 3.6 within one girl's (8.2) work, which is unified by two main themes – the conservation of natural resources and the modernization of manufactured resources.

Speech bubbles were used in the:

- Top right-hand corner – The mother is leaning into the bathroom to tell the child to take note of the time on the clock. The clock serves as an index to indicate succinctly that time is running out. The word bubble announces that in 'five minutes' the daughter should finish her shower to conserve water during the drought.
- Bottom left-hand corner – The girl is wearing special woollen clothing which, in the future, will be cool enough to wear even in the heat of summer. The word balloons say, 'It's not hot' and 'Yes it is' [but I don't even notice because of this new fabric].
- Bottom centre – The teacher at the front of the room has written a mathematical equation on the whiteboard. The whiteboard serves as an index to denote 'doing school'. The teacher is calling on the child by pointing to the student with the raised hand, asking her to answer the question, saying, 'Yes?'

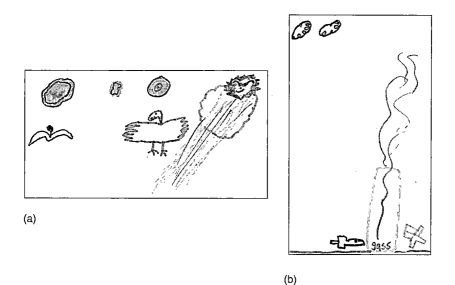

(a)

(b)

Figure 3.7 (a)   Descending Sun Rays [detail] (girl, 8.0)
Figure 3.7 (b)   Ascending Heat Rays [detail] (boy, 9.0)

Radiating and wavy lines were used to indicate that the water, lights and antennae were 'active', as in the:

- Top row, second column – water gushing from the bottom of the hose,
- Top row, last column – water spraying from the shower rose,
- Top row, third column – radiating light from the bulbs,
- Centre row, first column – radiating lines from the traffic light,
- Bottom row, first column – wavy heat lines surrounding the sun, and
- Bottom row, last column – radiating lines from the TV antennae.

The astute reader will pick up other examples of children's use of graphic devices presented throughout this book but not necessarily described in detail. Often these devices are a minor component within the artwork, such as in the examples given in Figures 3.7a and b of descending and ascending heat waves, which are extracted details from a girl's (8.0) and a boy's (9.0) drawings respectively.

An additional detail of a child's work in Figure 3.8 (boy, 4.8) illustrates how *whoosh lines* were used to move an object – a car – a technique that can also be applied to moving characters. Whoosh lines may be accompanied by gesture to bring the work 'alive', or, as in Figure 3.8, they may be supported by other graphic messages, such as the undulating road, which also implies action.

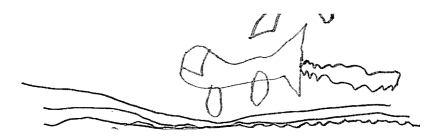

Figure 3.8   Car Whoosh Lines (boy, 4.8)

In sum, whoosh lines and wavy or radiating lines *animate* the frozen images within the still, 2-D format of drawing. Word bubbles *'audiate'* the silent action. In some ways, the *animation/audiation* of the artwork is similar to the intratextual interaction of film with soundtrack. Iconic speech bubbles and movement lines collectively contribute to the vibrant nature of the visual narrative. They reveal relationships and patterns, all of which contribute to the child's generation of meaning. Cartoon-like graphic devices such as these are 'articulated' (Metz, 1974, p. 242; 1981) with the objects, characters and events of children's artworks and with the language that they use to describe these. These signs interact in a complementary way within the holistic text.

Hence, the graphic representation of people, places, objects and events is not a static message. Indeed, there are many *implicit interactions* – object–object, object–people and people–people – that are denoted as dynamic events. In addition, interactions are revealed by the placement of objects and figures on the page, and the spatial relationships between these.

Spatial relations and meaning

Spatial relations in drawings are not semantically neutral. Instead, they carry some fundamental principles that influence our perception of how visual images are read. An intriguing issue is the question of whether, as a human species, we are predisposed toward interpreting ambiguous images in one way rather than another, through universal principles, or whether aspects of visual perception are learned and culturally variable. To explore this issue further, let us begin with a description of three *spatial syntagmatic* relations[1] (Chandler, 2002):

---

[1] A syntagm is a construction or sequence which functions as a relationship (i.e., linguistically, visually, spatially, temporally).

Figure 3.9   Swimming with Sister (girl, 8.6)

- in front/behind,
- close/distant, and
- above/below.

All three of these spatial relations are illustrated in Figure 3.9 (girl, 8.6), where two swimmers' bodies are positioned *front/behind* in a horizontal position, and *close* together. Yet there is a sense of depth or *distance* created between the swimmers and the viewer of the drawing: the waves near the swimmers are sharper and compressed, whereas the waves further from the action are flatter and expanded.

The three spatial relations also are communicated in Figure 3.10 by a young artist (girl, 5.0) who drew a person jumping on a trampoline. The large, main figure appears to be *close* to the viewer, and is captured in transition between airborne and landing – halfway between a vertical and a horizontal. This slanting orientation gives the impression that the body is in a dynamic state (Athey, 2007; Golomb, 2004). An impression of depth also is created through the significantly smaller striped trampoline and figure standing beside it, giving these the appearance of being in the *background* and *below* the main figure.

In front/behind and *close/distant* are communicated in another example (Figure 3.11) by a girl (8.3) who drew herself and her brother riding horses. These are illustrated through: (a) the differences in size of the riders and their horses; and (b) the upwardly undulating and gradually lighter surface of the grass area. In spite of these sophisticated elements,

Figure 3.10   Trampolining (girl, 5.0)

Figure 3.11   Horse Riding (girl, 8.3)

there are some anomalies in the drawing in relation to *above/below*. The multi-coloured shape in the right-hand section of the sky is a rainbow. To the left of this is a blue lake, which is meant to be interpreted as being in the distance (rather than in the sky). This rather common misplacement of things 'in the distance', as if seeing them above (or higher), is an issue closely linked to perception and children's developing ability to apply 'graphic rules' to depict meaning visually and spatially.

How spatial relations communicate meaning, linked to perception, is the focus of the field of Gestalt Psychology. According to Gestalt psychologists, there are several fundamental and universal features of human perceptual organization, and they claim that we may be predisposed towards interpreting images in certain ways according to these principles. Perhaps the most commonly known Gestalt principle is that of 'figure' and 'ground'. We separate a dominant shape, or 'figure', from the background or 'ground', as in the famous ambiguous figure which can be either: (a) a white vase on a black background; or (b) two human faces in silhouette facing each other on a white background. Some Gestalt principles of perception (Chandler, 2002, p. 87) that are relevant to the content of this chapter include:

- *Similarity* – features which *look similar* are associated,
- *Proximity* – features which are *close together* are associated, and
- *Surroundedness* – areas that are surrounded by other content tend to be perceived as *figures* – the figure is perceived as being inside or central, while the content outside is perceived as being on the periphery.

Each of these, or combinations of them, are described in greater detail in the following section.

Similarity and proximity

The example in Figure 3.12, of a girl's (5.0) drawing of family members and the family cat (right-hand side) includes figures that are in close proximity to show that they are part of a group. This is reinforced by the figures being equally spaced and similar in size and shape. Scarlet, the cat, is located on the far right of the cluster of sisters, differentiated from the others by four legs, but is as large (and implicitly as important) as the sisters. The mother is also large, standing at the door of the house, facing the children as they return home from school. The artist justifies her omission of her father in the drawing by saying, 'Daddy is inside, so I am not going to draw him. He's obviously in bed'.

Most of the content in this artwork is drawn in purple, with the exception of the orange sun, the thin blue skyline and the row of pink flowers aligned along the bottom edge of the paper. The tall, thin house, which contains several cross-hatched windows, is leaning inwards on a

Figure 3.12   Mother, Children and Cat (girl, 5.0)

left-to-right diagonal axis. The sisters and cat are aligned on a right-to-left diagonal axis, which provides balance to the overall text.

In a similar depiction by a 5-year-old girl, the schematic figures of the mother and three girls all had star-shaped dresses over stick-figure frames. Again, the artist did not include the father in her drawing, essentially because she did not know how to alter her female human schema to make it male. To explain this omission, she said, 'I don't know how to do Daddy's clothes. I won't put Daddy in this picture'.

Similarity, proximity and surroundedness

The drawing in Figure 3.13 by a 6-year-old girl also includes the clustering of similar-looking figures in close proximity (Golomb, 2004, p. 173) to symbolize that they belong together. This drawing is similar to the one presented earlier in this chapter (Figure 3.3), where the artist's M-shaped cloud complemented the shape of the first initial of the artist's name. In both artworks, the artists 'bound' the key subject of their drawings with a green groundline and a blue skyline to 'frame' the content. The ground and sky surrounding the figures make them appear to be inside and the centre of the focus.

Interestingly, one boy (5.0) circled key content in his drawing (Figure 3.14) to emphasize that certain things belong together as a unit. To illustrate the concept of family, the artist clustered himself,

Figure 3.13   Friends Together (girl, 6.0)

Figure 3.14   Family and Possessions (boy, 5.0)

his sister and his father in one circle, with the baby in a separate circle below them. In addition, he circled two prized family possessions – a tape-recorder and a car – and the dialogue below suggests that the artist realizes that these examples prototypically represent a larger range of things owned by the family.

> C: That's my sister, Anna and my Dad and … you can hardly see his [the baby's] face … I'll put a circle around him. I'll put a circle in the family, ok?
>
> I: What's in your family, a tape recorder and a car?
>
> C: I can't do all the rest [of the family possessions] because I know hundreds.

As a final example, surroundedness is a strong visual principle in Figure 3.15 by a 6-year-old girl. The bride, drawn in a central position within the church, is framed by the decorative streamers on the periphery of this space. The result is that the bride is presented as 'the nucleus of the information on which all the other elements are in some sense subservient' (Kress & van Leeuwen, 1996, p. 206; 1998, pp. 196–198). Two additional features help to focus the eye on the bride: the nearly symmetrical content inside the church (i.e., windows, streamers and pillars) and the colouring in of the background outside the main figure.

These examples provide compelling support that children consciously apply spatial principles to create meaning in their drawings. What is

Figure 3.15   Bride in Church (girl, 6.0)

not clear is whether children are predisposed to perceiving universal principles of perceptual organization (as Gestalt theorists believe), or whether structural perception is learned and culturally variable (as semioticians believe). Lakoff and Johnson (1980), for instance, argue that *orientational metaphors* are routinely linked to key concepts in a culture, which frame our experience. Two principles associated with this – vertical and horizontal axes – are described below in relation to one artist's work (which was discussed in Chapter 2 (pp 45–6) about people wanting to move to other planets).

Vertical and horizontal axes

Lakoff and Johnson (1980) claim that the vertical axis of visual compositions carries connotations: *up* is associated with *more* (e.g., goodness, virtue, happiness, high status, power, rationality) and *down* is associated with *less* (e.g., badness, depravity, sickness, low status, powerlessness, emotion). Kress and van Leeuwen (1996, 1998) emphasize that our reading of horizontal and vertical axes is influenced by how we have learned to read written text. This varies from culture to culture. In European cultures, for instance, writing and reading proceeds primarily along a horizontal axis, from left to right (compared to other cultures/languages, where the direction can proceed from right-to-left or top-to-bottom). Consequently, in European cultures, the 'default' for reading a picture would likely to be from left to right (unless attention is diverted by some salient features).

These principles are evident in the drawing in Figure 3.16. The artist (girl, 7.8) used prototypical images to describe several complex issues: the destruction of the forests; overpopulation, immigration and increased young parenting; and people moving away from Earth to live on other warm planets. Her minimalistic images were meant to stand for broad, universal ideas. She explained that the representation was deliberately sparse, to connote abstract, universal trends. These included:

- a single flower, a tree without branches and a leafless bush to represent the depleted rainforests,
- the male–female couple drawn in close *proximity* with similar features to represent the human race, in particular, young parents, immigrants and overpopulation,
- a planet to represent other places in space to which humans are moving, and
- a single person waving down from the planet, to stand for humans living away from earth.

Figure 3.16   Living on Other Planets (girl, 7.8)

At the more abstract level, her overall message connotes a range of concepts: greed, destruction and selfishness, but with an element of 'social wisdom'.

C: I think there's going to be more [people] because there's people that are very young, and they're having children. So I think they're going to grow up quicker than you and I. And people from overseas are deciding to come and live in different places.

I: And can you tell me anything about how you think people might um ... how people might treat other people when there's more people around?

C: Um, I think they might treat other people maybe, ah, a bit wiser than ... usual.

I: Moving onto the second part of your picture ... the ...

C: Forest.

I: Wow! You can hardly call it a forest, can you? What's happened to it?

C: Well, we don't have many forests in Australia now. And I think if we are gonna get more people it'll be ... like they'll want to make more houses and everything. So they'll ruin some of our land ... and forests and everything ... and we won't have many trees left, many bushes and flowers.

I: Well you ... your picture has got hardly any there ... is that what you mean?

C: Yeah. And most of it's dead ... the trees.

I: So you don't want people to cut down the forests and that ... but you think that will happen, because there'll be more people and they need those things.

C: Mmmm (*nods*).

I: And that ... what sort of effect will that have?

C: Um, I'm not really sure ... it'll kind of make it not the best place to live. And then I think people might stop coming, and everything.

I: And how do you think the people might feel about that ... you know, the er, loss of all their trees and stuff.

C: Um, I think some people might be very upset. And other kinds of people, they'll just be happy to have their houses and everything.

Kress and van Leeuwen's (1996, pp. 193–201; 1998, pp. 193–195) theory is applicable in this example. The vertical and horizontal axes of the work suggest a before-and-after temporal sequence.

The left/before and right/after axis suggests that: people's selfishness (left side) has lead to the destruction of the forests (right side).

The top/before and bottom/after axis also implies a temporal sequence. The *upper* part represents the abstract or generalized possibilities – the 'what might be' prospect of overpopulation and the destruction of the environment – which leads to the *lower section*, which represents the factual details – the 'what is' outcome, represented by a person waving from another planet after leaving Earth to live elsewhere.

The drawing has two parts and two themes, and the message functions as ideological – as a type of foretelling. This is reflected in the artist's prophetic style of language when she grapples with how to explain that her content is prototypic. I have added bracketed interpretations of her words, partly to review some of the terminology presented in Chapter 1, but also to illustrate the impressive knowledge that this girl was able to communicate about the power of drawing to symbolically express her thoughts and feelings:

• this kind of picture thing [visual text]...
• it's kind of showing [denoting through protypical signs]...
• it's trying to explain [connote a deeper meaning] ...
• that's what I tried to express [symbolically represent].

It is hard to not be struck by such powerful communication coming from a child who is not yet 8 years old. A similar prophetic style of message was communicated by another girl (8.6) when depicting an ill person, receiving medication. The artist commented that 'medicines and things like that will be different [in the future]. Um, I think that people will find a cure for things [diseases]'.

Messages such as these, and the visual-narrative way they are communicated, resurface the question raised earlier in this chapter about whether humans are *predisposed* towards creating and interpreting images in a particular way, or whether visual perception is *learned* and culturally variable. Nichols (1981) argues that visual perception and the ability to read images is learned, but that once we have developed the skill, it is easy to mistake it for an automatic or unlearned process. An analogous situation is how infants informally learn to speak through naturalistic interactions with their parents and others, which may appear so ordinary that it is considered innate and not shaped through informal scaffolding.

Likewise, children develop visual perception through informal learning, and come to use and interpret signs by applying systems of conventions. Becoming familiar with these systems requires sensitive perceiving and learning how to create and read visual text through practice, similar to how children learn to talk by practising speech. If children don't have opportunities to draw, they have reduced chances to learn the systems of graphic communication.

Like learning the systems of spatial relations in drawing, learning the systems of naming and labelling content and using graphic devices (e.g., speech bubbles and whoosh lines) are fundamental to young children's meaning-making. Through experience in drawing and exposure to visual media, children learn to read and write visual text, applying principles such as in-front/behind, close/distant, above/below, similarity, proximity and surroundedness. Children *employ* these principles, and the principles of vertical/horizontal axes, within their own works; they also learn to *interpret* these principles in the works of others.

Children informally (and sometimes formally) learn these principles when they watch film and look at posters, ads and other media. As in all areas of learning, children's ability to perceive and appreciate visual media is linked to their personal levels of exposure and the scaffolding they receive in learning how to read visual text. Likewise, children apply elements of graphic-narrative-embodied texts at varying levels when engaging in visual narratives, which is related to the type and level of practice they have had with this mixed media.

It should also be noted that there may be great variation in the 'sophistication' of individual children's visual narratives, even within one day. This variation is dependent on what it is the child wants to 'say' at a particular moment, his/her artistic intent at that time, and the form in which the child chooses to communicate this meaning.

Summary

The essence of young children's meaning-making is a richly inte- grated creative act that includes many *signs* – words, graphics, sounds, writing, gestures, postures – which stand for or *represent* other things. These signs conform to tacit *rules* that involve multi- ple *channels* of communication (e.g., visual-spatial, auditory and bodily-kinaesthetic), and frequently there is a crossing of these var- ious channels.

In addition, children's meaning-making fluidly shifts between *intra- textual* components. Their graphic-ing of objects and events is anchored by the use of labels, speech bubbles, whoosh lines, captions and other techniques. These components function symbiotically – they are written and read as relationships within the text. Similar rela- tionships are created through spatial features, such as in-front/behind, close/distant, above/below, similarity, proximity and surroundedness.

Children learn and apply these intratextual features through exposure to visual text and experience with graphic media. Hence, visual narratives are a discourse that liberates children to 'say' that which cannot be said as easily through words alone. This is one reason why art is a fundamental medium for surfacing the meaning- making and creative competence of young children. Art should take a central position in early childhood education – it is a core component of children's learning, knowing, representing and communicating.

Reflections

As emphasized in this chapter, children's use of intratextual features such as letters, words and graphic devices is linked to the artist's intentions and the artwork's purposes and functions. Consequently, amongst the collection of drawings compiled by you and your col- leagues, there may or may not be some examples of children's incorporation of intratextual features in their works.

1. Review the drawings that you collected in relation to Chapter 1 and the visual narratives collected in relation to Chapter 2 to see

(Continued)

(Continued)

if there are examples of the following, and discuss the meaning that was communicated intratextually:

    (a) Naming or labelling,
    (b) Speech bubbles or whoosh lines,
    (c) Prototypes to stand for generic concepts.

2. Focus your attention on the spatial relationships in the children's drawings. Identify and discuss examples of meaning with your colleagues in relation to:

    (a) In front/behind,
    (b) Close/distant,
    (c) Above/below,
    (d) Similarity,
    (e) Proximity,
    (f) Surroundedness,
    (g) Vertical axes,
    (h) Horizontal axes.

Additional readings

Kendrick, M., & McKay, R. (2004). Drawings as an alternative way of understanding young children's constructions of literacy. *Journal of Early Childhood Literacy, 4*(1), 109–127.

Kress, G., & van Leeuwen, T. (1998). Front pages: (The critical) analysis of newspaper layout. In A. Bell and P. Garrett (Eds.), *Approaches to media discourse* (pp. 186–219). Oxford: Blackwell.

Short, K.G., Kauffman, G., & Kahn, L.H. (2000). 'I just need to draw': Responding to literature across multiple sign systems. *The Reading Teacher, 54*(2), 160–172.

Siegel, M. (1995). More than words: The generative power of transmediation for learning. *Canadian Journal of Education, 20,* 455–475.

Drawing and Embodiment

Figure 4.1 Shooting a Criminal (boy, 7.8)

At the completion of this chapter, you should be able to:

1. Describe enactive, iconic and symbolic modes in more detail,
2. Understand how children engage in these modes while drawing-telling,
3. Reflect on how individuals learn to write and read messages that are communicated through these three modes.

As described in the previous chapters, fundamental processes of drawing involve representing the world and capturing reality through experience, imagination and reasoning. This chapter goes on to focus on how embodied concepts play a central role in these processes.

Such a description cannot take place without acknowledging the work of Jerome Bruner (1986, 1996). Bruner described how the learning processes of young children involve internal reorganizations of previously known ideas. This begins with the manipulation of materials and moves increasingly towards abstract thought. Such thought processes involve three distinct modes of reasoning – enactive, iconic and symbolic. Each of these modes will be elaborated in detail in this chapter in relation to children's meaning-making while drawing.

Bruner believed that each mode is present and accessible throughout development, but some modes are *dominant* during particular phases of life (Hollyman, n.d.). For instance, it is notable that young children often can learn to play a musical instrument more quickly than an older person who is just beginning. This is because learning through action is a fundamental way of knowing for young children, whereas thinking and abstract reasoning are often considered to take precedence in adult lives – although examples in the previous chapter, in particular, and further examples in the remaining chapters provide evidence of young children's abstract thinking through visual narratives. The dominance of the enactive mode is most striking as seen in the case of musical prodigies who, at very young ages, are able to perform on musical instruments and recall complex musical passages at the level of accomplished adult musicians.

This chapter will delve deeper into how children's enactive engagement is also evident in their visual narratives. It will show how, through opportunities to manipulate art materials directly, children's thinking and reasoning is enhanced, which is why art is such an important medium for children's expression of ideas and feelings. I aim to elaborate on how drawing is strongly associated with spatial and physical awareness – it is *thinking through action*. It involves developing three kinds of skills, which are closely linked:

- *enactive* skills (representing thoughts through motor response),
- *iconic* skills (comparing and contrasting mental images of objects by transforming perception into meaning), and
- *symbolic* skills (reasoning abstractly and employing culturally-based symbols).

Many examples will be provided to illustrate children's meaning through drawing, using these three modes.

Figure 4.2 Tumbling Blocks (boy, 5.2)

The Enactive Mode

Let us begin with a brief discussion of how very young children's learning relies extensively on enactive skills. Babies and infants learn through their actions when they roll over, move their limbs, sit up and manipulate objects. They begin to represent events through motor responses that lead to some predictable result. An infant, for instance, derives enormous satisfaction from repeatedly performing some action (Gross, 1973), such as dropping objects from his/her highchair over and over again and watching the trajectory of each as it falls to the floor.

Similarly, the photograph in Figure 4.2 captures the pleasure that one 4-year-old boy experienced by repeatedly setting up blocks that were interlinked so that the 'lead' block created a domino effect, ultimately causing the stacked blocks at the end to collapse. He set up this configuration several times, taking great delight as the tower crashed to the floor.

Athey (2007) argues that 2–5-year-old children work on particular patterns of repeatable behaviours, referring to each of these patterns as schemas which pervade children's actions and speech as well as their mark-making. Through such schemas, 'experiences are assimilated and gradually coordinated' (Athey, 2007, p. 50). Athey maintains that children's learning can be developed by following their intrinsic schematic *forms of thought*, their interest in elements from their surroundings and their own intrinsic motivation (which must be facilitated by materials and support from adults).

Young children engage in such schematic processes when they draw, by practising particular marks with great intensity and concentration. The rehearsing of circles and other shapes, and schema of people, places, objects and events becomes the basis for exploring and perceiving slight variations in graphic signs. This helps children perfect their messages, leading to more complex forms of representation.

Such learning through drawing has strong association with play, playfulness and creativity. Through play, children portray thoughts and emotions by example, such as capturing the feelings of nurturance through movement and the use of props and other resources (e.g., embracing and comforting a doll). Play provides the necessary sustenance for children to *transform reality* (Chandler, 2002).

Likewise, the intrinsic satisfaction that children get out of playfully manipulating graphic messages helps them build new structures and knowledge (Dewey, 1934/1988). The act of drawing integrates *sensorimotor* and other forms of thinking, reasoning, feeling and learning, which emerges through the 'thinking body'. This is known as *somatic* meaning-making. Somatic knowing involves exchanges between the psyche (mind), the soma (body) (Ross, 2000) and the 'soul' (Best, 2000a, 2000b).

Through somatic meaning-making, knowledge is held in the child's body as a somatic artefact (Dewey, 1934/1988). For instance, children project their somatic knowledge when they feel a lump in their throats when an actor cries, or when they respond emotionally to an artwork, music or dance. Their feelings are triggered by some subconscious association held within their bodies.

Neurological research (especially in primates) has explored the mirror neurons found in the pre-motor cortex and their integral role in somatically-modelled learning. As Humphrey (2006) elaborates, these neurons:

> become active both when the subject performs a particular action – grasping a nut by the fingers for example – *and* when he sees another individual doing the very same thing, raising the strong possibility that there may be 'sensory mirror neurons', in other words neurons that link the observation of someone else having a sensation to the execution of a similar sensation oneself. (pp. 104–106)

Empathy, or the ability to imagine yourself in someone else's position and to intuit what that person is feeling, is a fundamental component of the arts. Empathy is the 'ability to stand in others' shoes, to see with their eyes, and to feel with their hearts ... and because it requires attuning oneself to another, empathy often involves an element of mimicry' (Pink, 2006, p.159). Pink elaborates that the mode of the emotions is nonverbal and the 'main canvas for displaying those emotions is the face' (p. 163).

Somatic meaning-making is *performed* as children play and draw. When playing, for instance, a child mimics the roar of an engine while rolling a toy truck across the ground. The coordination of voicing and pushing the toy allows the child to 'be' the truck through sound and movement through space. Likewise, while drawing, children play with the characters they draw, and embody the events within their artworks.

As mentioned in Chapter 1, the act of making art, for the 4–8 year-old children described in this book, is creative play, which originates in the child's imagination. Indeed, Matthews (1999) writes that 'play is implicated in the development of all forms of representation' (p. 24). Children, in their art and play activities, are exploring ideas which allow the world to be seen in new ways. Thus the young child's 'recreation of a 'real' life experience may, in fact, contain an element of invention or fantasy' (Bhroin, 2007, p. 4).

In such activities, there is a *dominance of the somatic over the cerebral* (Callery, 2001). In other words, knowledge is grasped through body-based engagement. As Lecoq (2000, p. 9) puts it, 'the body knows things about which the mind is ignorant'. This is part and parcel of all forms of competence that require physical skill, such as acting, sport, playing a musical instrument or creating art. When it boils right down to it, somatic knowledge is fundamental to all human thinking – it is the *basis* of knowing.

As discussed in Chapter 1, the dramatic scene in children's visual narratives is not always figured analogically through spatial or pictorial means, but may be indicated gesturally (as in mime), or through expressive vocalisms (as in radio drama). The young artist is performing perceptual experiments in his/her own mind and probing the emotional self through felt responses to images and perceived relationships to others. Barber (2008, p. 3) describes this as 'a means of direct metaphorical communication, and a way of somatically involving oneself in perception' via the materials of the drawing medium, and by 'investing these materials with (or discovering within them) the capacity to physically embody the self'. Put more directly, drawing is a form of thinking and awareness that is deeply rooted in the body. Barber (2008) claims that the greater the range of physical movement and muscle use that the artist has personally experienced, the better his/her ability to internalize and, via the act of drawing, embody the poses or movements of the figures being depicted.

More broadly speaking, such sensorimotor learning becomes a part of the neurological system (Lakoff & Johnson, 1999, p. 20), and as a result, it can seem natural, unconscious, unlearned. For instance, we engage in cross-channel thinking-feeling when we visualize a thought before the words come, or see an image and sensory connections and emotional memories come flooding back to us. Indeed, the language that we use reflects this. We know, for example, what is meant when someone says that they were made to feel 'small' with humiliation, or felt 'weighed down' with care, 'stiff' with fright, 'light' as air or 'depressed'. Metaphors such as these help us understand one thing in terms of something else. George Lakoff argues that metaphors are central to reason (Pink, 2006, p. 139). They communicate our emotional states. Metaphors are grounded in bodily experiences, linked to *time* and *space* (Lakoff & Johnson, 1980, 1999). Indeed, as Twyla Tharpe (2003, p. 139) claimed, metaphor is the 'lifeblood of all art' (Pink, 2006, p. 136).

Young children, in particular, use metaphoric language to reflect their experiences. Kress (2000b) provides an example of a 3-year-old's language while attempting to clamber up a very steep, grassy slope. The young boy said, 'This is a heavy hill', using a bodily-kinaesthetic kind of system to express something like 'it is really hard; really heavy work for me to climb this hill' (p. 155). Because he didn't have the word 'steep' in his vocabulary, he used the term 'heavy' – it was the most apt word to describe the physical energy required to climb the hill. This type of verbal expression is cross-modal – the meaning from the physical mode 'slips over' to the verbal mode. Kress (1997, p. 29) elaborates that 'the move, the transduction across modes, encourages the synaesthetic potentials of the child in their transformative, creative actions' which 'offers an enormous potential enrichment, cognitively, conceptually, aesthetically and affectively'.

Visual metaphor is used in art through elements such as lines, points, shapes, values, colour and texture. Children assemble these basic visual signifiers in their texts to make meaning and to produce sensations that carry emotionally undertones or connotations, metaphorically. As examples of this, I draw upon Danesi (2007, p. 112) who explains that *value* – the darkness or lightness of a line or shape – plays an important role in the portrayal of contrasts, such as 'dark' vs 'light'. *Colour* conveys mood, feeling and atmosphere which is reflected in metaphoric terms such as 'warm', 'soft', 'cold' and 'harsh'.

The *texture* of wavy lines, for instance, tends to produce a much more 'pleasant' sensation compared to angular lines, which can connote 'agitation'. Finally, *lines* and *shapes* are combined compositionally to create 'depth' (i.e., perspective) and illusions of three 'dimensions'. Danesi elaborates that such visual devices elicit various sensory modalities in tandem, intermodally. Like Kress, Danesi (2007) uses the term synaesthesia to characterize this phenomenon – that is, one sensation is evoked by another, as 'when a loud noise produces the image of a blinding light, or vice versa' (p. 112).

Children easily cross modes in artistic ways: colours evoke moods; lines of verse stimulate a dance or a song; motions of the hand suggest lines of poetry. 'As readily as an adult associates one word to another, so easily do most children cut across domains and categories, often realizing unanticipated (and powerful) metaphors in the process' (Gardner, 1980, p. 99). This is because children do not differentiate between poetry and prose, narration and drama (Linqvist, 2001). 'Battle lines' have not been formed around the media of art, music, dance and drama.[1] Indeed, children seem to realize intuitively that elements of rhythm, balance, composition and harmony are shared by arts media (Gardner, 1980). So a child's composition in one art form (e.g., drawing) often can stimulate a related activity in another form (e.g., dramatization). For instance, children frequently dramatize the actions of their drawn characters, or demonstrate the movement of depicted objects, such as in these examples:

> I was doing this like that (*demonstrates dance steps*) and tripped over and got a scar (girl, 7.9).
>
> She is going to do some tap dancing at the wedding (*demonstrates*) (girl, 6.3).
>
> I'm playing with the fish (*stands up*). We get a piece of string and this fish flaps around (*demonstrates*) (boy, 5.1).

At other times, children's somatic engagement with their artworks may be more subtle. For instance, one boy (8.0), after drawing an elaborate mansion, role-played the responses of the owners of the house when seeing it for the first time:

> When they looked at it first, when they were going to move in, they thought, 'wow!'. Like their mouths opened like ... (*demonstrates*).

---

[1] Unfortunately, as children progress through the school system, the individual arts become increasingly separated and specialized, which is counter-intuitive in relation to children's natural proclivities.

Another boy (8.0), when drawing Olympians receiving medals, clasped his hands to mimic receiving these awards. Responses, such as these, are linked to our *sense memory*, which is an experience-based building up of a bank of memories and associations. Sense memory plays a big part in our capacity to imagine and empathize. Rabiger (2008) elaborates on this issue in relation to acting and film directing:

> Memories and sensory input are intimately linked – the smell of baked potatoes at home, the flapping of one's clothes at the seaside, the rough feel of rope in a gym, the song of a skylark rising ever higher into an azure sky – all these sensory memories are key to a time, place, mood, and special people. An actor reading a script relates his or her character's experiences to whatever correlated in his memory bank. Then, he finds the analogous experiences to help imagine what a pilot does while losing control of an aircraft, what a store clerk does as she wins the lottery, or what a pensioner does on finding that he's lost his door key. (p. 220)

Creativity and synaesthesia rely on all of the senses when we make meaning. The artefacts children make in their visual narrative texts, which are composed of words, movement/gestures and graphic marks, reflect synaesthetic activity. In early years, creativity and synaesthesia are in full bloom in the types of texts children create and the materials they use to create them (Pahl & Rowsell, 2005). Pahl and Rowsell (2005, pp. 13–14) lament that, 'as our schooling progresses into the junior and intermediate years, creative expression or synaesthesia activity changes, and there is far more ... privileging of the written over other modes'.

Kress (1997) also emphasizes the importance of synaesthesia activities in young children's learning, which give rise to specific forms of thinking. Synaesthesia involves 'different kinds of bodily engagement with the world – that is, not just sight as with reading, or hearing as with speech, but touch, smell, taste, feel' (pp. xvii–xviii). He makes an argument that such thinking and feeling should be fostered in education:

> In our thinking, subconsciously or consciously, in our feelings, we constantly translate from one medium to another. This ability, and this fact of synaesthesia is essential for humans to understand the world. It is the basis of all metaphor, and of much of our most significant innovation. We may want to foster rather than suppress this activity. (Kress, 1997, pp. xvii–xviii)

Visual narratives foster synaesthetic responses in children because embodied, graphic and verbal concepts work in consort. As Gardner (1980, p. 99) describes this, they 'share certain expressive facets'. This is illustrated in the drawing at the beginning of this chapter (Figure 4.1), where the man's falling from the building was accompanied by the artist's downward *gesture* of his hand, in sync with a dramatically vocalized 'ahhhhhh', descending in pitch and fading in volume. The *dotted lines* show the bullet coming from the gun, hitting the man on the roof; the *dashes* show the victim's fall from the top of the building (the victim is shown twice – before and after the fall).

As illustrated by these examples, children incorporate art into their bodies. They extend their senses, imagination, emotion and aesthetics through the use of the tools of the drawing media. Other examples given below show how the body was used to express ideas and feelings through: gestures that describe the movement of objects or figures; marks that leave traces of an object's movement on the page; finger movements that enact characters or events; and page-lifting to represent things floating in outer space.

Gestures to describe events

Children's explanations of graphic actions, through gesture, are similar to animating a cartoon. For instance, one preschool boy, who drew a car going along a road, ran his pen across the bottom of the page to 'animate' the car's movement. Another boy traced the path of a car moving along an arched monorail track. In cases where children trace the trajectory of the movement, the gesture implies, in one quick movement, the graphic equivalent of dots and dashes.

For instance, in Figure 4.3 the girl's (6.0) depiction is of a koala that has been run over by a car, which includes gesturing along the length of the page to explain this event:

Figure 4.3   Koala Crossing the Road (girl, 6.0)

> He [koala] was trying to go ... (*traces the length of the road, left to right, with her finger*) to the gum leaves. *Draws leaves at the end of the road.*

The koala's pathway from the left-hand to the right-hand side of the road was described verbally and mimicked gesturally to explain the outcome – the death of the koala, mid-way between these two points.

Children's gestures and language also can refer to content that is not drawn but is implicit within the artwork's theme (Golomb, 2004). For instance, in *North Brisbane Roadworks* (see Chapter 3), the artist (5.7) said, 'The school is just over that way' (pointing to a location off the page). The artist (5.9) of *Driver Training* (see Chapter 2) referred to a shopping mall that was located off the page: 'They are driving into the shopping fare' (gestures along the road). Similarly, one girl (6.6) said that her house was 'over the mountain', and pointed to the sky in her drawing, but said that she would not draw the house because she couldn't 'rub it out' [it wasn't pertinent to the theme, and would destroy the composition].

These examples illustrate that children are aware of spatial relationships between what is within (and often, what is outside) the frame of the page. They are conscious that the drawing is like a photograph. It cuts across some of the objects rather than including them as a whole, inviting the viewer to 'fill in the gaps' (Jakobson & Halle, 1956). It suggests that what is being offered is a 'slice-of-life' (Chandler, 2002, p. 133).

Gestural marks

Gestural representation (Wolf & Perry, 1988) is one of the earliest systems that children employ to symbolize certain movements and events. Matthews (1999) referred to this as 'action representation'. Bhroin provides an example of this, where a preschool child 'almost relived the storm as he drew this picture, making banging noises with his crayon, reminiscent of the sound of hailstones. "That's the snow coming down from the sky and that's all the cracking on the ground and the stones"' (Bhroin, 2007, p. 14).

Art derives its unique power from the fact that emotional content may be embodied in its *formal* qualities such as the child's 'banging' gestural marks described above. The direct link between perception and embodiment also is shown in older children's use of gestural representation when they iconically show speed through the use of whoosh lines following a moving object. Smith (1982) described such experiences as a complex blend of objective and expressive qualities, which stems from the interplay between thought and feeling. An excellent description of the expressively somatic blend of content and form is offered by Barber (2008) when describing professional adult artists:

> Just as a skilled and experienced violinist unconsciously presses down, draws, and eases up with the bow in a fully, physically engaged sensitivity to the emotional potency of sound, the artist presses, lifts, and draws the charcoal across and into the page in a visually traced re-experience of the act of touch. (p. 12)

Barber emphasizes that such embodiment is directly experienced engagement. It is not only a mental act, but a physical one. Both psyche and soma are essential functions of all arts disciplines.

Matthews (1999) described young children's perceptual-physical acts – a child's physical movements, his/her trail of the brush on paper and the movement of imaginary objects – as compressed into the *visual-motor* act of creating. In such cases, the child's graphic marks represent two aspects (Athey, 2007):

* *configuration* (e.g., the external appearance of something, such as a car), and
* *movement* (e.g., the operative components of the car, such as spiralling across the road).

An example of this configuration–movement relationship is illustrated in the opening artwork to Chapter 6 (Figure 6.1), where the boy (8.5) drew the skid marks of car tracks (at the door to the high rise building), synchronized with the vocalism of an 'aaaaahhhhh', descending in pitch and fading out. His futuristic cars, which are powered on grass (bottom, right and central) have green whoosh lines behind them (sourced from 'grass stations' on Earth). But when two cars spiral out of orbit (top, left-hand side) one car is given a red whoosh line, and the artist says, 'the car used to be powered on grass, but now it is *powered on down* because it's so *heavy*'. His expression 'powered on down' is another example of cross-modal meaning between physical and verbal modes, similar to the child's description above of clamoring up the 'heavy hill'.

The blending of *configuration* and *movement* is further illustrated in Figure 4.4 in a preschool boy's (5.4) drawing of a remote control car (top left). His work includes a complex description of several interconnecting wires to make the car 'run': 'And I will show you how much wires are in there'. The remote control is drawn on the right-hand side of the page, with two circles (knobs, marked '|' for on, and '–' for off) and two wires that converge toward its pointer at the bottom of the page. Two wires extend from the remote control tip, one which connects to the back of the car and the other to its front wheel.

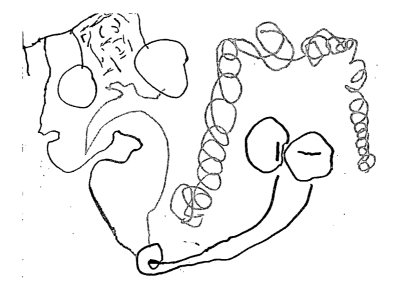

Figure 4.4   Remote Control Car (boy, 5.4)

> And that little knob connects to the little strong bit around there [back of car]. The little wire connects to those wheels so it can move, and that wire goes into the wheel and makes that top wheel move.

Near the tip of the pointer, the artist enacts the spiralling movement of the car, creating an inverted U-shaped pattern. 'You move it [remote control]. This is going to be a curly thing. It goes in circles [spirals].' Then, he looks at his trace-of-movement and sees another image – a clown's curly hair (spiralling pathway), the clown's eyes (the circles containing '|' for on and '–' for off) and the clown's long nose (the remote control's wires merging to the tip).

C: Do you know what it is? I know what it is – curly hair.

I: So what's the curly hair for?

C: Do you know what? I've got clown hair. It's curly, but it's all different colours. Funny curly hair! Yeah!

The boy's use of the words 'Do you know what?' functioned as a transition point. It marked a shift in theme, announcing that the text was about to be 'read' in a new way.

Similarly, gestural marks were used by a girl (4.7) to link objects in a theme of 'being caught in a rainstorm and flood' (Figure 4.5). The person [she] is framed by a dark line that takes on the contours of the body, similar to a raincoat, surrounded by numerous rain dots. The pink 'love hearts' (around the borders of the page) function as

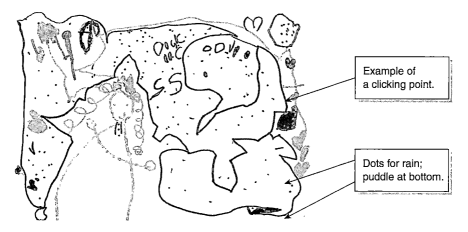

Example of
a clicking point.

Dots for rain;
puddle at bottom.

Figure 4.5   In the Flood with Love Hearts (girl, 4.7)

balloons, which need to be 'clicked together' to lift the person into the air, away from the flood.[2]

> C: The love hearts have to be clicked together. *Draws a line connecting the love hearts (right-hand side of the page).* Otherwise it won't take me anywhere. Click ... click ... click *(vocalization of the drawing actions).* Gonna click everything. *Continues the line across the top of the page, stopping at each 'clicking' point to connect the love hearts.* Click ... click. Clicked everything.

> I: Clicking together are they? What are they clicking together for?

> C: 'Cause they want to take me up to the air. They're carrying all the balloons up into the air, and people. See these dots, they're the rain. They come down to here [puddle]. Lots of water everywhere. So I sort of should get out of that place.

The clicking of the hearts/balloons is enacted graphically through a *connecting action on paper.* It is similar in spirit to the earlier photograph of the 4-year-old boy's pushing of the end block in the series to create a domino effect (Figure 4.2). The balloons' collective lifting resulted in carrying the girl away from danger. Then the young artist draws herself a second time as a small figure in profile (top, left-hand quarter of the page), with a line connecting to the pink cloud. This dual-representation of herself functioned as a before-and-after event, bringing closure to the theme – safety.

---

[2]Perhaps her use of the term 'click' was associated with computer mouse clicks, which she may have learned through digital games involving clicking and connecting objects.

Using fingers

Children often counted the appendages of drawn figures or the number of objects or people in their drawings. For instance, one child drew a figure's hand, and counted '1, 2, 3, 4, 5', pointing to each drawn digit consecutively. Another girl counted on her fingers while saying, 'And there's lots of children. 1, 2, 3, 4, 5, 6, 7. There's seven children'.

Others used their fingers to enact the movement of machines or people. One example comes from the work discussed in Chapter 3 (see *Reuban Backhoeing*, Figure 3.5): 'This is a small machine because it's got a digger at the front (*puts hands out like a tray*) and it's got a little digger on the side'. His visual narrative included both action and direction:

- circular lines in the ground to show the energetic results of the machine's work on the dirt, and
- the upward orientation of the stairs, with Reuban stepping up the incline.

Reuban was aware of how the scale of the drawing was smaller than real objects, saying, 'It's going to be a big shed. It's gotta be a little drawing it will'. In addition, the stairs of the house represented only part of the house. 'And I have to have a big green house. And I had to go off this thing [the page] because I didn't have enough room'. This focus on only the stairs at the entrance to the house is similar to how a close-up photograph features the subject, framed in the centre of the shot – Reuban, walking up the stairs. The disproportionate size of Reuban compared to the backhoe functions like a blow-up (i.e., a detailed focus).

Reuban then used his fingers, as if they were the drawn figure's legs, and 'climbed' each tread. This action was accompanied with the repeated word, 'step step step ... ' voiced in synchrony with his finger movements. He then said, 'I'm going to make a tunnel into the house too', and pushed his thumb into the paper, as if it were the front digger of the backhoe, breaking up the dirt. Reuban's spatially-based description of how he could move through the tunnel in the event of a fire illustrates his ability to understand an idea without having to experience it directly.

> R: The machine has gotta drill a hole ... it's gotta be a hole digger (*pushes his thumb into the paper*). And I've gotta push it like that, and it's gotta be into the case under the stairs. It's gotta go dig ... dig ... dig ... dig ... dig. (*Uses his thumb to 'dig' across the bottom, under the grass, and then under the stairs, to where the tunnel comes out.*) And there's where you can walk up.

I: Why do you need a tunnel?

R: So I can get out and in if I want to *[looks surprised at the question]*.

I: Can't you just walk around, straight across?

R: Well the house might catch on fire and I'll be able to go here *(points to the bottom of the tunnel)*, because the fire mightn't be there. And if it gets the door broken, then I can just tunnel back in there *(points to the shed)*.

Finally, Reuban added details to the figure on the stairs, saying, 'Look at the way I'm saying goodbye [waving] to someone'. This gesture signalled the close of the theme and a type of farewell to the interlocutor at the end of the drawing-telling interaction. In sum, Reuban's configuration, movement and language were synchronized and interacted symbiotically in two, enacted events – backhoeing and stepping – see Table 4.1.

Table 4.1   Configuration, Movement, Language: Backhoeing, Stepping

	Backhoeing	**Stepping**
Configuration	the *graphic* depiction of the backhoe doing the digging	the *graphic* depiction of the person doing the walking
Movement	the *action* of digging into the paper with the thumb	the *action* of walking up the stairs using his fingers
Language	the descriptive *words*, 'dig, dig, dig ...'	the descriptive *words*, 'step, step, step ...'

A final example of a child's use of his fingers is by a 5-year-old boy who drew himself and his mother 'looking, smiling, throwing rocks and digging holes' (Figure 4.6). The rock in the figure's right hand touches but is not contained within the hand (Golomb, 2004). However, the left hand 'holds' the diamond (which he found near the waterfall and is giving to his mother, to 'make her rich').

Similar to the before-and-after example above, of getting away from the flood, this artist depicts himself and his mother in two places: (a) on top of a mountain (large and in the foreground); and (b) down by the waterfall (small and in the background). The boy showed remarkable spatial, graphic and verbal ability to juxtapose the foreground and background in terms of height, distance and size. The figures simultaneously were in 'full-shot' and 'long-shot'.

See, this [foreground] is where we climbed up. It's [mountain] about as high as Brisbane. See it's [background] all very small, because we're very far away from this mountain, so it's very small.

Figure 4.6   Me, Mum, Diamond and Waterfall (boy, 5.0)

While the artist enacts the events of his artwork, he alternates between 'zooming' in on the figures at the waterfall and 'pulling-back' to the scene in the foreground. In the process, he uses his fingers to show how he will cross to the other side of the waterfall.

> I'll go over to the other side to Mum (*moves his fingers inside the waterfall area, 'stepping' only on the white parts*). And all the white bits are dry land. That's how Mum got on the other side. She was standing next to me and then she walked around the water.

His movement of fingers, to 'step across the stones', is an example of how children internalize actions of what their own bodies would do. This boy's psychosomatic awareness and application illustrates how drawing involves reflecting a mental state, depicted on the page. Barber (2008, p. 11) argues this is more than 'muscle memory'. Rather, he claims that 'there is something anciently evolved and deeply physical going on when we draw'.

Compositionally, in the waterfall-mountain drawing, the eye is drawn to the figures in the foreground. Yet, the artwork functions as three events – first we are here, then we go to the waterfall where I find the diamond, and then we 'pose' with me giving the diamond to my Mum. The content and form of this artwork were psychosomatically expressed, where in the child's mind or mental state, he 'went' to these locations and enacted these events, showing remarkable graphic skills to depict concepts of time (a sequence of events) and space (perspective: distance/foreground).

Lifting the page

A final example in relation to the *enactive* mode of drawing is illustrated in Figure 4.7 to show a remarkable case of how one boy (5.4) embodied the paper itself and used many other gestures to demonstrate sophisticated concepts: gravity, intersecting computer wires and the separation of component parts of the spaceship. The drawing-telling was titled, *In Space in a Rocket*, and the artist said, 'I'm really into all this stuff [about space]. It's good'. He commented that he had watched a video with his family, and that he often practices 'being in a space rocket at home' by using his couches.

Figure 4.7   In Space in a Rocket (boy, 5.4)

He begins by drawing a space rocket in the top, left-hand side of the page. Its blackness, compared to the whiteness of the page, stimulates a conversation about quickly passing from night to day, while travelling in outer space, and the engine power of the spaceship.

> I think it will be a little black [in space]. It's going to be a little bit black ... then it gets lighter and white as you come through space. This is a space rocket that goes very fast, because it has a very lot of engines. *Adds a point*

to the front of the rocket. It has one engine, two engines, three, four, five … it has five engines. But when it's in space, it just has three engines [it drops two, described later].

He talks about what the astronauts see in space – stars, the sun, the moon and Earth.

They're stars *[four, near the rocket].* And then there's even a sun in space. *Draws the sun in the lower, right-hand section of the page.* Like, they [astronauts] just saw it. They look in their big mirror and they don't know for sure what they see, so they … so they think … the sun's the Earth. I made the beams on the sun.

Then, he gestures and describes how the moon looks like a crescent when shadowed by Earth.

Draws a crescent moon below the rocket. It's half the moon. Very half *(laughs).* And the moon looks like a question. That's because the world is turning … like the question *(makes a crescent shape with his arm and rotates it).* 'Cause the more the world, it turns, the more stranger the moon looks.

Then he draws a second rocket (central, left) and adds jet streams behind it and the other rocket. The number of jet streams is based on the number of engines of each rocket.

This rocket is different-er than the other one. Because it doesn't have the engines. *Adds one jet stream at the back.* It just has one [engine]. *Adds three jet streams to the large rocket.*

The gravity of this rocket pulls it too fast down [to Earth]. It crashes in the water. But … it doesn't <u>crash</u> in the water. It has three parachutes. *Draws Earth with several continents, near the second rocket.* Green is the world – that one is the world.

Then he plays an 'Eenie Meenie Minie Mo' type of game to determine which one of the rockets he would 'be', using symbols – the numerals 1 and 2 and a tick and a cross – to label this selection-rejection process.

I don't know which space rocket I'm going to be … the three-engine, or the one-engine? I must mark it. I think I'll just … 1-2-3-4-5-6-7-8-9-10 *(Points back and forth between the two rockets as he counts).* I'll be in the little blue space rocket … so I'll put down number one. *Writes '1' on top of the blue rocket.* And this one can be … a cross … and it can be number … two. *Adds a cross and a '2' to the black rocket.* And this one can be … tick. *Ticks the top of the blue rocket.* I'm in that one.

When describing components of the artwork, the boy demonstrates how there is no gravity in outer space.

> Do you know there's even fuel tanks floating around in space? *(Gestures, with pen in hand, 'floating' the fuel tanks in space.)* And I'll draw the fuel tanks now *[below the second space rocket].* They're circles ... and there's the road to another fuel tank ... and another one to another fuel tank. And that fuel is for anything in space. But it has to be flame proof, or ... the fuel tanks will explode.

Then he adds a space station 'house' and a computer-operated shuttle that sends up satellites.

> And there's even a ... little house in space. *To the right of the fuel tanks he draws six purple rectangles joined with lines.* There's gravity there ... but you can't ... move about ... too easy *(uses hands and arms to gesture actions).*

> And there's another space rocket, but there's no people in here. This space rocket is computerized. *Draws a large space station on the top right-hand side.* That's where they sit the shuttle. These are just satellite senders. And you can send up satellites and things.

The artist describes the prospect of the rocket on the space shuttle crashing if it is not controlled by the computer. He embodies many concepts by intersecting his fingers, lifting the page and gesturing.

> The computer is ... that part *(points to the top of the space shuttle).* And there's all sort of wires ... they join things up *(intersects his fingers to illustrate 'joining').* But you can't see inside it because there's all balancing stuff *(uses two hands to lift the paper off the desk to demonstrate balance).*

> A very ... skinny ... remote-controlled satellite spaceship goes up with no people, just a computer. It breaks off the fuel tanks *(gestures breaking off).* And the fuel tanks could crash, and explode ... into that one [space shuttle] or that one [house]. But there's a computer in there to drive the space rockets, and to work the satellite thing.

Then he demonstrates how the capsule of the large rocket drops its early-stage engines and breaks away by thrusting its remaining engines. This event is described as using gigantic scissors to cut a rope. A green mark is drawn to represent the severing of the engines from the capsule.

> And it [space capsule] floats around like this *(lifts and warps the paper to show floating).* And the ropes are just around ... up there. Could put a mark ... a green pen mark. *Adds a mark left of the numeral '2' on top of the large rocket, to represent cutting away.* So you can cut off that rope with

some scissors and it snaps off. And then this part just floats, staying on the same spot. And it has to fire its three main engines … and it has to try to work away to get the satellite going.

Finally, he describes how the satellite relays a distress signal to a helicopter to rescue the rocket that fell into the ocean (using its parachute to avoid crashing).

It's [satellite] going to send [a signal] … it sends to a helicopter. 'Cause it throws … *(gestures)* a boat throws a little candle [flare]. They send it out there in the water … and it floats *(gestures)*. And the satellite sends to a helicopter. And it could save somebody's [the pilot's] life.

This 5-year-old boy depicted several sophisticated concepts about outer space: computers, stars/sun/moon/Earth, space rockets/shuttles/ stations, communications and gravity. He embodied these ideas by:

1. demonstrating with his arm the shape of the moon, and how the Earth's shadow changes its apparent shape,
2. using the numerals 1 and 2 and a tick and a cross to label the selected rocket,
3. marking the severing point where the engines break away from the capsule,
4. using a pen to demonstrate how the fuel tanks float in space,
5. gesturing what it is like for the astronauts to move round in the space station,
6. intersecting his fingers to show the joining of computer wires,
7. lifting and warping the paper to show how things balance in space, and how the fuel tanks float while the capsule pulls away, and
8. gesturing throwing the flare for the helicopter to see the crashed rocket.

Through the enactive mode, this artist's 'thinking body' was somatically aligned with his graphic meaning-making. His meaning was enhanced by the use of several *iconic* signs – graphic marks and physical demonstrations with pen, paper, finger and arm movements. These allowed the boy to compare and contrast *mental images of objects and events* and to elaborate these through language. Iconicity (i.e., the making of iconic signs) worked symbiotically with words to create meaning, more powerfully than if these components were separated. The importance of iconicity in children's drawings is significant. Hence, the next section focuses on the iconic mode in more detail.

The iconic mode

Icons have been used throughout history to communicate ideas succinctly. They have played a significant role in the evolution of pictorial and written communication. For instance, going back over 30,000 years, the early inscriptions, cave drawings and pictorial signs of prehistoric civilizations show evidence that pictographs, ideographs and hieroglyphs played an important role in early sign-making cultures. These iconic signs resembled the objects and actions to which they referred, either directly or metaphorically. The making of iconic signs is 'evidence that human understanding is guided initially by sensory perception ... put simply, humans tend to model the world as they see, hear, smell, taste, and touch it' (Danesi, 2007, p. 42). Over time, picture writing became more symbolic and less iconic (Gelb, 1963), possibly because letters, numbers and other symbols came to be seen as being more flexible and efficient (Lyons, 1977, p. 103).

Nonetheless, iconic forms of communication continue to serve an important function today, particularly when linguistic interaction is limited. Icons are found in many sources, such as: the 'trash can' and 'cursor' in the graphic user interface system employed on computers; the 'male/female' signs on washroom doors and the colours blue and red on washroom taps; and diagonal lines through circles to indicate 'no smoking', 'no parking' and so on. Danesi (2007, p. 41) defined icons as 'signs that have been constructed to resemble their referents in some way'. Photographs, portraits or Roman numerals, for instance, are visual icons because they resemble their references in a visual way.

Yet, despite their name, icons are not necessarily visual. An icon can also feel, sound, taste or smell like the concept it represents. Danesi (2007) describes olfactory icons (perfume which imitates natural scents), gustatory icons (food additives which simulate the taste of natural foods) and tactile icons (a block with a letter of the alphabet carved into it, which can be figured out through the medium of touch). Sensory-kinaesthetic types of icons were demonstrated by the artist described above when he imitated the feeling of floating in space by lifting the piece of paper and 'warping it'. Such iconic representations depend on visual or other sensory association. *They transform perception into meaning, economically* by resembling or imitating an object or event (or possessing some qualities or properties of the object or event) (Pierce, 1931–1958, 2.276–7).

This section illustrates two types of icons: (a) lines or dots that connect or separate figures or objects; and (b) vocalisms, such as repeated words

Figure 4.8   Robbing a House (boy, 8.5)

and onomatopoeia. However, as with all examples in this book, it should be noted that the child's choice to incorporate icons in his/her drawing-telling is closely aligned with the *purpose* of the communication, and how this is intended to *function*. Hence, the same child may use icons in one drawing, but not in another, created only moments later.

Lines and Dots to Connect or Separate Things

As discussed in Chapter 3, whoosh lines behind a moving object/figure represent motion iconically, by imitating or graphically *animating* the action. Similar movement-based icons were presented in the artwork at the beginning of this chapter (Figure 4.1) – dots and dashes showed the trajectory of the bullet and the victim's fall from the building.

Another example is provided in Figure 4.8, where a boy (8.5) drew two themes:

- Rising gas waves depicting pollution [a detail of this component was presented in Chapter 3]: 'That's a bird, and that's a plane, and it crashed … 'cause there was too much pollution, they couldn't see'.
- Connecting lines depicting a burglary: 'The sun's not out, all the clouds are out, and all the crime's come in because some people are in shops. And I'm going to do the person doing the crime into the house, because there are not that much jobs [people are

unemployed]. People is breaking into your houses and it gets really scary, because you don't know who it is'.

Makes a long line, connecting the man's hand to the door knob of the house. Like they go into other shops, and steal all things what they need. *Adds a red shape in the other hand of the man to stand for stolen things.* Because they might not get any money, because of [lack of] work ... and they have to go out and steal. *Puts green dots [money] on top of the red line in the man's hand.*

Connecting icons also were included in the girl's (5.7) '*I'm* gonna ... *she's* gonna grab the gun off him' drawing of a police officer handcuffing bad people (Figure 2.4). 'There's one handcuff. I'm going to put it on that one [the man in the centre] and [on] the other one ... here [the man on the left].' The handcuff in the right hand of the police officer touches the edge of the bad man's gun. But the handcuffing of the second criminal is iconically represented by four dots drawn above the suspended handcuff. Facing the cognitive challenge of how to handcuff the criminal outside the police officer's reach, the artist 'floats' the second handcuff in a dynamic position, as if in a right-facing, forward direction. The dots above the handcuff suggest a continued right-directional movement, a sort of looping-around-the-back-of-the-page concept, to reach the man on the other side.

These examples illustrate how icons were used to connect things. But icons can also be used to separate things, as in the space age artwork described above, where a mark represented the 'severing' of the engines from the capsule of the space rocket so it could break away. Similarly, in a detail of the drawing shown in Figure 4.9, the boy (6.7) includes a line between two underground tunnels, to prevent the ants (dots) from getting to the worms (squiggly lines):

A worm house [centre]. There's an ant place here [right of the worm house] and another ants' place [far left]. The ants are trying to get into the worms' house. *Draws a separating line between the worm and ant houses to keep the ants out.*

In sum, iconic signs help children organize and communicate information spatially and somatically. The functions, forms and purposes from the examples illustrated above and reviewed from previous chapters are set out in Table 4.2.

Dots and lines communicate relations between objects, and often express and evoke emotional responses (Gross, 1973). Sometimes this emotional connection can be reflected in children's language, which may include the use of repeated words or onomatopoeia.

Figure 4.9 Ant and Worm Houses [detail] (boy, 6.7)

Table 4.2 Function, Form, Purpose: Connection, Separation

Function	Form	Purpose
Connection	Dots between the gun on the ground and the man on the roof	To shoot the criminal
	Dots above the police officer's handcuff	To capture the felon around the other side of the page
	A line between the burglar's hand and the doorknob	To break into the house
	Lines to click love heart balloons together	To lift the girl to safety
Separation	A line above the space rocket	To sever the connection between the engine and capsule
	A line between the ants' and worms' tunnels	To block the ants' entry

Repeated words and onomatopoeia to give emphasis

Danesi (2007, p. 43) defined *vocalism* as 'the use of sounds to model something through imitation or resemblance, or to emphasize or call attention to something'. For instance, in Chapter 2, the boy who drew the family picnic and elaborated on the concept that children have more 'live', used *increasing loudness* and *lengthening* when he said that 'kids are *more* ... moooorrre!' Other children's expressiveness was shown in relation to their use of *repeated words* to accompany their graphic actions, such as 'step, step, step' (going up the stairs) or 'click, click, click' (joining love hearts). Repeated words are iconic in that they transform perceptions into meaning by accentuating some aspect of the child's narrative to give more impact, such as:

He's got great big sleeves. Fat, fat, fat, fat sleeves.

And the house has ... a very very big ... very very big ... bedroom.

Sometimes children used repeated words to emphasize their graphic actions, such as when colouring the ceiling of the hospital ('colour, colour, colour'). Other examples included increasing or decreasing the rate of speech during vocal delivery in order to convey urgency, or the

Figure 4.10   The Future Rock Star (boy, 6.5)

opposite, placidness. An alternative expressive form of linguistic communication that children used was *onomatopoeia* – a vocal imitation
of the sound associated with something or its action. Onomatopoeia is
similar to sound effects in radio drama. For instance, while drawing a
lorikeet, one girl (8.3) imitated the sound of the bird. Another girl (6.7)
while describing a mousetrap said, 'and we put some cheese on it, and
the mouse runs in, and eats it, and then it goes **plff** (accompanied by a
gesture simulating the rapid slamming of the trap's jaws)! And they're
dead. Chops 'em in half'.

In the example shown in Figure 4.10, a boy (6.5) wrote and vocalized the guitar music coming from the fold-back speaker at the bottom of the stage – 'Dnnn DDDDTTRM'. Near this lettering is his title
of the work, *One Man Jam*. He surrounded this writing with radiating
lines, to suggest sound waves. Then he commented, 'I wish I could
put this [music] on the computer, and then I would go **drrrr**' (*gestures
playing the guitar*). The artist's use of icons for sound, imitative gesture
and radiating lines worked in consort. As he gestured playing the
instrument, he simultaneously created the sound; the radiating lines
are a graphic artefact of the music that was created.

Similarly, a girl (5.8) used onomatopoeia to describe the office chair in
her drawing (Figure 4.11), saying, 'It swivels around, *grrrrrrrr*' (*gestures a
spiralling movement with her hand*). Her use of onomatopoeia was close to

Figure 4.11   Working in an Office with Swiveling Chair (girl, 5.8)

her direct perception, which is reflected in her statement that the spinning 'makes you all dizzy'. The artist's sense of playfulness within the work-based context of an office is also reflected in her comments about games versus work, and the role of computers in the future:

> I like computers, I like playing on them, but I don't like doing work on them. No way. But I can see in the future that games will be turned into work, and work will be turned into games.

These examples illustrate children's fluid integration of the *enactive* mode (representing thoughts through motor response) and the *iconic* mode (transferring mental images into meaning through lines, dots, repeated words and onomatopoeia). Similar integration occurs when children engage in the *symbolic* mode. This mode generally involves 'big picture' ideas and the use of symbols that are understood 'universally'.

The symbolic mode

A *symbol* is a sign that stands for something in a conventional way. For instance, a maple leaf stands for 'Canada', a tombstone for 'death' and white for 'purity'. Children learn that symbols operate under some form of system. In language, for instance, children must learn words, vocabulary, letters and punctuation marks. Mathematics consists of learning symbolic operations, such as classifying things, and making series, connections and combinations – much of which is understood through the coordination of actions. Similarly, children must learn to read visual symbols, such as road signs or traffic lights, and symbolic signs, such as *emblems* (flags, a school logo) that indicate membership or ownership.

Symbols such as these become *associated* with general ideas. They are interpreted as *referring to* particular objects. The emblem of a flag, for instance, particularly when combined with the singing of an anthem, can generate a sense of national affiliation. Such responses are socially learned. Consequently, children's ability to use symbols is dependent on their learning of particular cultural codes. Social semioticians are particularly interested in the conventional codes that govern human social life, such as the rules of interaction, which include haptic codes (shaking hands) or language codes ('Nice to meet you') and so on. Social semiotics 'anchors us to the study of situated practices in the construction of identities and the part that our engagement with sign-systems plays in such processes' (Chandler, 2002, p. 218).

There is insufficient space within this book to go into how art texts are products of social and historical processes or how the various codes associated with art specify the ways in which art elements are combined to create texts of various kinds (e.g., maps, diagrams, portraits, landscapes). However, for the purposes of briefly illustrating the symbolic mode, some examples below illustrate how symbols were incorporated to communicate meaning, which were linked to the children's understanding of socially learned, conventional codes.

Flags, medals, uniforms and levels

The artwork in Figure 4.12, by an 8-year-old boy, symbolized the various nations represented at an Olympic event, and included national flags and athletes' uniforms. His symbolization of 1st, 2nd and 3rd place winners included these numerical terms to label the relative positioning of the athletes in the event, plus the following:

- a tiered podium,
- flags flown at different heights, and
- different coloured uniforms and medals.

The artist's awareness of symbolism, where the highest level stands for the best (as in the tiered podium), is reflected in his language when he is discussing the flags:

Figure 4.12   Olympic Medalists (boy, 8.0)

The person who came 1st is the highest flag. This is Australia, so Australia's flag goes up the highest. Then Canada is the 2nd highest flag. And Great Britain came 3rd, so Great Britain is the 3rd highest.

Other children's language indicated that they understood the role of symbols in communicating meaning within their artworks. For instance, the girl (6.0) who drew the swivelling chair included a description of how her Park Ranger uniform must be brown (compared to the uniforms of other occupations).

C: My Dad's clothes are brown so I will colour my clothes brown too. I'm going to be a ranger like my Dad. And I can be a Princess when I grow up. And be a ballerina as well. A ballerina dancer.

I: Is this when you are a ranger is it?

C: Yes, because I don't look like a ballerina, because I'm not in pink.

Traffic lights, zebra crossings, numbers and arrows

Several symbols within one drawing are illustrated in Figure 4.13 in a girl's (8.7) depiction of a city:

- two *traffic lights*, one at the zebra crossing (with green and red *icons* of walking people) and another in front of the bus (with red, yellow and green light icons),

- *numbers* at the top of the lift on the building (with the *index* of an arrow to indicate 'going up'), and
- the *word* 'school' (with an arrow on top of the building, to indicate 'that way').

Likewise, two symbols are used in Figure 4.14, to ward off unwanted guests: the skull and crossbones on the gate and the sign on the fence

Figure 4.13   The City (girl, 8.7)

Figure 4.14   Mr Grouch's Castle (boy, 8.0)

('Dager, Dager' [danger]). The artist (boy, 8.0) explained these by saying, 'The man, Mr Grouch, doesn't like children coming in, so he put that up to try and scare them away'. Right of the gate is a secret garage door (dotted, to show that it is 'invisible') so that the driver can avoid people by using his fast car: 'He saved up for a Ferrari, so no one can see him ... he just zooms up the street'.

As illustrated, children's drawings may include symbols, which are encoded forms of culturally-learned communication. Numbers, written words, flags, signs and other symbols can amplify children's meaning. In addition, children's verbal descriptions may give further clarification, such as in the example above, where the artist uses increased volume and repeated words to describe Mr Grouch's frustration with the fruit bats that destroy his trees: 'Every day he goes out to the hill and sprays the trees with some water so the fruit can grow back. But it doesn't. The fruit bats <u>just</u> come back and back and back'.

Summary

This chapter illustrated that often the enactive, iconic and symbolic modes co-exist as children draw-tell. Examples are summarized in Table 4.3 to illustrate the forms and functions of children's meaning-making within these three modes.

The symbiotic relationship between the enactive, iconic and symbolic modes assists young artists in their development of conceptual understanding and meaning-making. Learning how to be skilful, multimodal communicators can be influenced by children's imagination, creativity and developmental ability. But learning is also influenced by children's exposure to a range of enactive, graphic and narrative texts – a matter that will be discussed in greater detail in the following chapter.

Table 4.3   Mode, Form, Function: Enactive, Iconic, Symbolic

Mode	Form	Function
Enactive: representing thoughts through motor response	Gesture	To imitate playing a guitar or spinning a chair; or to explain the shape of the moon in relation to the Earth's revolutions
	Traces of movement left on the page	To show a car's spiralling track marks
	Counting in an eliminative way	To select a preferred spacecraft

Table 4.3   (Continued)

Mode	Form	Function
	Finger or thumb movements	To enact a machine digging in the dirt, a person walking up stairs or a person stepping across the waterfall
	Lifting the page	To demonstrate floating and balancing
Iconic: economically resembling mental images of objects and actions	Lines or dots	To connect or separate objects to stand for breaking into a house, handcuffing a criminal or keeping ants out; or to represent an 'invisible' door
	Repeated words and vocalisms	To accompany an enactment ('step, step, step'), give the narrative more impact ('fat, fat, fat, fat sleeves'; the fruit bats just keep coming 'back'; kids are mooooorrrre!) or to emphasise a graphic action ('colour, colour, colour') or an embodied action ('step, step, step'; 'dig, dig, dig')
	Onomatopoeia	To imitate the sound of something or an action (**grrrr** to spin a chair; **drrrr** to play a guitar)
Symbolic: employing culturally-learned symbols that operate within a system	Flags, uniforms, numbers, medals, podium levels; traffic lights, zebra crossings; skull and crossbones	To represent 'big picture' ideas that are understood 'universally', such as nationality and winning; road safety; or a warning against danger

〰 Reflections

1. Representing the world, or capturing reality through experience, is a significant component of art. This takes place in three ways:

    (a) *enaction* (actions portray or depict thoughts and emotions by physical example),

(Continued)

(Continued)

    (b) *iconicity* (icons succinctly stand for generic meaning, such as male/female, and provide a conceptual understanding of how we operate in the world), and

    (c) *symbolizing* (symbols, such as flags or numbers, are encoded signs that represent abstract ideas).

Reflect on these categories in relation to your personal experiences of how you represent and understand the world in your daily life. Collect examples of visual messages from sources such as ads, posters or photographs, and discuss how icons and symbols are read.

2. Revisit the children's drawings-tellings you collected in relation to Chapters 1 and 2. Look for examples of enactive, iconic and symbolic representation in these artworks (and transcriptions of words, vocalisms and gestures) and discuss these with your classmates.

Additional readings

Callery, D. (2001). *Through the body: A practical guide to physical theatre.* New York: Routledge.

Gross, L.P. (1973). Art as the communication of competence. Paper presented at the Symposium on Communication and the Individual in Contemporary Society. www.ucalgary.ca/~rseiler/grosslp.htm

Hollyman, D. (retrieved 27 July 2008). Jerome Bruner: A web overview. http://au.geocities.com/vanunoo/Humannature/bruner.html

Intertextuality:
Borrowing with a Personal Stamp

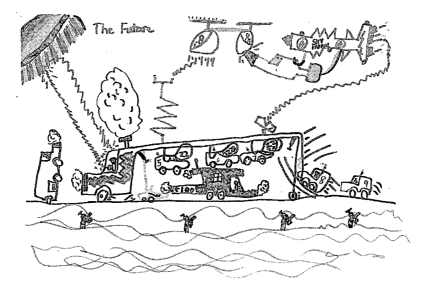

Figure 5.1   Semi-Taxi and Sky Patrol (boy, 8.0)

At the completion of this chapter, you should be able to:

1. Understand that children deliberately create visual and temporal structure in their artworks, often by borrowing from other texts,
2. Describe the textual features of children's drawings and how they are similar to the texts of film and theatre, and
3. Reflect on how children's visual narratives may consist of scenes, which are like free-form episodes centred on characters and associated events.

I want to begin this chapter by making links to how authors of children's books, songs, theatre and film frequently embrace children's interest in repetition through the use of visual, narrative, melodic or plot reiterations. For instance, a character in a children's book might pass through several locations and 'discover' new things along the way, all of which are conceptually linked to a central theme. A friend and colleague of mine, Madonna Stinson, commented to me that such pattern repetition establishes a predictable plot thread, and slight variations in the content provide unexpected but 'safe surprises' that appeal to children. Children's desire to spot the variation in repetition establishes a sort of 'do it again' expectation for a new surprise to come.

This inherent search for structure, particularly through experiential action, seems to be an underpinning aspect of human cognition. Likewise, structure is a fundamental aspect of children's visual narratives. To recap on some issues from Chapter 1, young children enact experiences on paper, imaginatively creating characters, objects, places and events, the plot themes of which are conceptually linked. This involves layers of visual action and running narrative working in harmony, simultaneously. A child's visual narrative is similar to play, but because it is a solo effort, it affords the child the freedom to become a 'cast of one', simultaneously taking on multiple roles – artist, scripter, narrator, performer, director, audience, critic. The child can 'be' all of the characters, select when and how to play with all the available 'voices' and develop the plot/theme, layer the action and alter the scenery at will.

The content of these playful encounters often seems to be embedded in the themes of a collective youth culture and may follow some of the conventions of popular media. Indeed, with the extensive exposure that today's children have to a range of texts, such as films, comic books, computer games and TV/DVD, it is not surprising that these texts provide contexts for children to create their own, new texts while drawing. The boundaries between various genres today are quite fluid and are becoming increasingly blurred. As Chandler (2002, p. 200) points out, blended genres have been given recent coinages such as 'advertorials', 'informercials', 'edutainment', 'docudrama' and 'faction' (a blend of 'fact' and 'fiction'). This blurring of boundaries between texts is called *intertextuality*. The animated TV programme *The Simpsons* and films like *Shrek* or amusing contemporary ads are 'particularly self-conscious forms of intertextuality' that credit audiences with the necessary experience to understand that the text is alluding to other texts (Chandler, 2002, p. 200). These appeal because they tap into the world of lived experience. Indeed, often children incorporate phrases from these texts into their own speech and interactions.

It is not difficult to identify instances within children's artworks where the popular media seems to have influenced children's thinking and visual narratives. They may 'borrow' from popular texts when drawing, yet each child's version of 'reality' and depiction of other-worldly reality carries a personal imprint. Children infuse their own meaning and make wilful choices about their content and how to depict it. Similar to how a film maker might draw upon myths and legends as a starting point, children borrow ideas and expand these within their visual narratives. Other texts help children frame their own ideas, by seeing life through an alternative prism. Such is the nature of intertextuality. It involves re-visioning, and borrowing, while giving new texts a personal stamp.

Some children were conscious of the role of intertextuality in their artworks, acknowledging the sources that inspired their ideas. For instance, John's (pseudonym) (6.6) comments below (in relation to an artwork that will be described in more detail in Chapter 6), were stimulated by a number of concepts that he had picked up from the science-based TV programme, *Beyond 2000*, which was the inspiration for the title of his artwork – *Beyond 2050* (Figure 6.5). John applied an idea from this programme to imaginatively depict a domed roof over a city.

> Most of these things I've seen in *Beyond 2000* and everything. But [in that programme] they don't tell you much about beyond 2000. They just tell you, say, if you're making a big glass net the size of a school, they'll tell you it'll be ready by a certain year and everything. So this [dome over the city] is just – I haven't seen this before – I made it up.

John was also conscious of the influence of film and television on people's imagination and thinking, and expressed a concern that some people might distort facts as a result of watching science fiction:

> Some people say they've been abducted by aliens, just 'cause the movies came out. Why couldn't they tell us earlier, before the movie came out? 'Cause I've seen the movie too. I think they're just telling us, for us to get scared.

The artist's drawing was influenced by science fiction and other film genres. These genres are often rooted in mythical themes (e.g., heroes battling against evil) and fantasy (e.g., fairies). Myth and fantasy provide a safe place for children to come to terms with their hopes, fears, wishes and concerns. While making their own artworks, children can grapple with ideas and emotions *symbolically*. Their themes might include conflicting, frightening, dark or taboo depictions about anger, abandonment, injuries or jealousy, and dualistic concepts such as love/hate, birth/death, aggression/kindness or poverty/ wealth. Many writers provide rich examples of children's visual portrayal of concepts like struggles between good and bad, powerful and powerless or cruelty and kindness, which may be resolved through victory or righteousness (cf. Dyson, 1997; Golomb, 2004; Wilson & Wilson, 1977, 1979).

While drawing constructs such as these, the child is in control and can shape the fate of the characters and the determinants of power. Indeed, sometimes children improvise and deliberately violate conventions, just for the joy of it. As they construct their characters, objects, places and events on paper, layers of content and relationships begin to emerge. This stimulates certain types of problem-solving and structures. In the process, the child becomes his/her own audience and critic and selects the 'best' methods for depicting particular thoughts and feelings. In many ways, the processes and outcomes have properties that are like features of film and theatre.

Filmic and theatric features in children's visual narratives

The textual features inherent in children's visual narratives, like that of film and theatre, include:

- characters with signifying functions (e.g., postures, expressions, gestures), linked to their roles, personal qualities, behaviours and goals,
- objects, places, settings, times, sceneries and decors and associations with these,
- speech, actions and subtexts of depicted characters, and
- structure – the flow of information, articulated in space and time (e.g., themes, plot, events and sequences).

These aspects allow the young artists to bring their works 'alive', similar to how a film director works with various elements to create a 'movie', or how an actor depicts a character in a 'play'. In some ways, observing a child engaged in graphic-narrative-embodied play is metaphorically like being there with the characters on a film or theatrical set, observing the director's techniques of capturing the action as it occurs. Although a filmic framework is not literally applicable to a child's art-based play, there are figurative equivalencies. Clearly, a child is not using a camera to shoot the content of the drawing, but aesthetic decisions are being made in the selection, execution, framing and reframing of ideas in relation to matters such as:

- light (day/night) and colour (bright/dull),
- sound (telling the content; using expressive vocalisms and onomatopoeia),
- action (gesture and iconic devices such as whoosh lines),
- time (compression, flashbacks and flashforwards), such as cutting between scenes,
- space (front/behind, close/distant, above/below), orientational metaphors (vertical/horizontal axes), size differentiations and foci (e.g., close-ups, in the distance), and
- structure (verbal, visual, spatial, temporal), which generally is multilinear and integrated.

The structure, or order in which events are told, results from the nature of the child's plot and his/her authorial intentions, which often change as the child spontaneously 'edits' the evolving visual narrative. In many ways, children's unfolding images are analogous to the filmic features of frames, shots, scenes and sequences. These terms will be briefly defined and then elaborated throughout this chapter to illustrate comparable elements within children's works:

- *Frame* – a single image or smallest compositional unit of a film's structure, captured on a strip of motion picture film, similar to a still photograph. A frame can also be referred to as a *still* – such as a photogram for a finished film or a publicity shot of an actor or a scene,
- *Shot* – the basic building block or unit of film, which is a single, constant take made by a motion picture camera, uninterrupted by cuts or editing,
- *Scene* – usually a shot, or a series of shots, that together comprise a single, complete and unified dramatic event, action or plot within a film (much like an act in a play). The end of a scene is often indicated by a change in time, action and/or location, and
- *Sequence* – a composition of scenes.

Children's artworks incorporate elements of time and space that are similar to these filmic devices. Drawing on the classic study of Hodge and Tripp (1986, p. 20), *Children and Television*, I will illustrate how four underpinning syntagms were applied in children's visual narratives, either discretely or combined:

- *same space* (syntopic),
- *different space* (diatopic),
- *same time* (synchronic), and
- *different time* (diachronic).

The technique of depicting 'same place and same time' is the simplest syntagm and is similar to a frame or a shot. More complex structures, such as 'different place and different time', have elements that often are similar to a scene or a sequence. Examples from children will illustrate these syntagms, starting from the simplest and moving to the more complex works.

Same time, same space

Many of the children's drawings appear to be quite static, resembling a still photograph, and these I will call *photo-shoot drawings*. The relatively static impression given is largely attributed to the frontal orientation of the figures. The characters face outwards, as if posing for a photograph. To use an analogy to film, the artwork functions similar to how the cast inside the drama is looking out and the audience are outside looking in.

Golomb (2004, p. 66) explains the economy of frontality from an aesthetic standpoint, stating that it: (a) captures the most characteristic attributes; (b) maintains the artwork's symmetry; and (c) provides maximal information with minimal effort. Frontal orientation may occur, even when the figures are meant to be interacting or when a figure is depicting action involving an object. Rather than facing the direction of the interaction, the figure is looking directly out at the viewer (or analogously, the camera). For instance, in Figure 5.2, the boy (6.0) drew himself mowing the lawn, but the figure is not looking at or touching the lawn mower.

Similarly, the example of a girl (5.5) (Figure 5.3) playing with her dog is stagnant, yet the eyeline and body and limb direction of the figure is slightly orientated, diagonally, toward the dog, suggesting a chasing type of interaction. Kress and van Leeuwen (1996) and Jewitt and Oyama (2001) refer to eyeline and body orientation as *vectors*, which connect characters with each other or a character with an object.

Vector-based depictions are similar to a freeze frame, where the characters' gestures capture action as it happens. In the *freeze-frame drawing* in Figure 5.4, the boy's (6.0) dramatic action is described: 'there's some cars going along and there's a man holding up a stop sign. I'm waving to the person who's holding the stop sign'. Although the figure in the foreground is waving to the person behind him, both

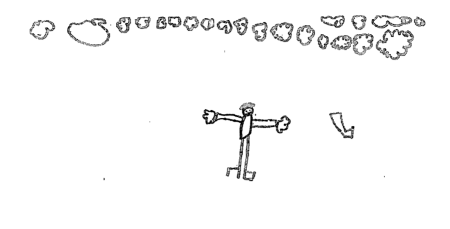

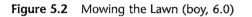

Figure 5.2   Mowing the Lawn (boy, 6.0)

Figure 5.3   Chasing the Dog (girl, 5.5)

figures are oriented to the viewer of the artwork rather than toward each other. Although this may seem 'socially incorrect', the artist seems more interested in creating a sense of perspective by positioning the man holding the sign in the background, and smaller. In addition, the receding lines on the zebra crossing give a sense of depth.

Figure 5.4   Road Workers Waving (boy, 6.0)

Figure 5.5   Blind Man with Dog (girl, 6.0)

In the artwork shown in Figure 5.5, the angle of the man's body suggests 'energy' and a pulling back of the dog on the leash, halting him at the stop lights. The girl (6.0) symbolically used stars to represent the eyes of the visually disabled man walking with his guide dog. She narrated other action without illustrating it graphically, such as pressing the buttons on the stoplight pole to make the traffic stop.

These examples centred on a single event, occurring in a single place and time. Yet drawings may include more than one event occurring at the same time and place, linked through a central theme. It is worth revisiting the 'road works' example from Chapter 3, which illustrates:

(a)   (b)

Figure 5.6   Storyboarded Events

(a) a bobcat spreading coal on the road; and (b) children crossing the road to go to school. These two events function as separate but unified *stills* occurring simultaneously. If storyboarded,[1] they would look like Figure 5.6a and b.

Yet, when artworks depict content occurring in the same space but at a different time, or at the same time but in a different space, the spatial-temporal content tends to be more complex. These two syntagms are described briefly with reference to artworks shown in previous chapters.

Same space, different time

An example of two different events occurring in the same space was shown in *Driver Training* (Chapter 2, Figure 2.8), where the boot of the car served two different functions. It originally contained groceries which the man is taking out (scene one); later the boot contained a battery which the man turns on to light up the driver-training sign (scene two). It was not necessary for the artist to draw these as two separate scenes, because the body position of the main character remained constant. The change of scene was marked by the narrative, rather than graphically.

---

[1] A storyboard is a series of illustrations or stills (sometimes with captions) that provide a synopsis for a film story or a complex scene.

Same time, different space

The examples below are works that implied different spaces within the same time frame. Children's descriptions of these spaces were presented like verbal 'side stories', but the content was not elaborated graphically, such as:

- *Fairy and Secret Garden*, where the artist made reference to beautiful things inside the secret fairy house (Chapter 2, Figure 2.7),
- *Horse Riding*, where the artist mentioned animals and resources on the farm and children swimming in the lake (Chapter 3, Figure 3.12), and
- *Mother, Children and Cat*, where the artist referred to Daddy who is inside the house, sleeping (Chapter 3, Figure 3.13).

Different time, different space

The most complex depictions, which warrant more detail, were those that showed more than one scene occurring in different spaces and at different times. The *Road Works* example above would not fall into this category, even when storyboarded as two separate stills, because the spatial and temporal aspects occur simultaneously. But the example shown in Figure 5.7 by a boy (5.7) contains sequences of time across different spaces.

The artist drew himself three times, to show that he is getting bigger as he gets older. The three figures are different colours and have increasingly smaller heads and longer arms and legs as they 'grow'. As the finale to the work, the artist drew himself a fourth time, when he is an adult, employed as a driver of a crane. Of the two cranes depicted, he is in the one on the right, and his brother, who is already a crane driver, is in the crane on the left. Reading from left to right (Kress & van Leeuwen, 1996), the time and space sequence implies a storyline of: 'My brother is older and bigger and works as a crane driver. I am still small, but when I get big, I will also work as a crane driver'.

Other examples presented earlier in this book contain more than one still occurring in different spaces within the artwork, such as:

- a man (a) planting a flag on the earth and then (b) going for a ride in his spaceship (Chapter 1, Figure 1.1),
- the boy (a) driving a backhoe and then (b) walking up the stairs to his house (shown in Chapter 3, Figure 3.5 and discussed further in Chapter 4),
- people (a) on Earth and (b) moving to other planets (Chapter 3, Figure 3.17),
- a man (a) being shot and then (b) falling from the top of a building (Chapter 4, Figure 4.1),

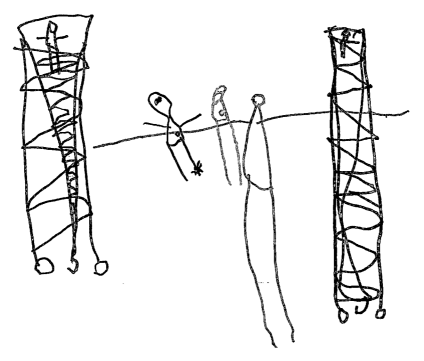

Figure 5.7   Crane Drivers (boy, 5.7)

- a girl (a) caught in the rain and then (b) lifted to safety (Chapter 4, Figure 4.5), and
- a boy and his mother (a) going to the waterfall and then (b) back to the top of the mountain (Chapter 4, Figure 4.6).

Perhaps the most complex, dynamic and elaborated example of a child's depiction of two different places and two different times is the artwork described in greater detail below, entitled *The Olympics and the Police Place*. This work includes several frames and scenes.

The Olympics and the Police Place

Ethan's (6.4) dual-depiction occurred on two different continents – Australia and some other non-specified place in the world. Like many children who live 'down under', Ethan was conscious of how much of the world, being several hours behind Australia, was 'dark' while Australia was 'light'. Hence, Ethan drew a line between the left-hand side of the world to differentiate it from the other side. He used many techniques to shift between two spatial-temporal planes,

Figure 5.8   The Olympics and the Police Place (boy, 6.4)

and to bring one side of the world 'awake' while the other side was 'sleeping' (see Figure 5.8).

On the left-hand side, in the rectangle taking up the top one-third of the page, Ethan depicts an Olympic event (a topic which was of interest to many children as the games were to take place close to the time that the children were drawing their works). The Olympic scene includes two *prototypical* athletes (one red, Canadian; one green, Australian) running around a track. Ethan explains that 'the Canadians are coming second, and the Australians are beating the Canadians'.

Possibly for the sake of creating a riveting tale (e.g., tension between good and evil, victories and defeats, heroes and villains), or perhaps because of an awareness of terrorism occurring at the Munich Olympics, Ethan included a bomb explosion in this scene, which is depicted by red, jagged lines arching above the track and green, jagged metal exploding above this. 'That's where the bomb came ... and that's all the metal things that came up.'

Ethan demonstrated flexibility of thought as he grappled with how to illustrate, on one page, two separate events occurring on opposite sides of the world. The difficulty he faced was associated with the fact that he wanted each of the scenes to occur during the daytime, but cognitively he knew that when it was daytime on one side of the world, it would be night on the other side.

His dual depiction of events actually began on the right-hand side of the page, which is a complicated police station scene (discussed in

Figure 5.9   Fading the Sun In, Out and In Again [detail]

more detail later in this segment). Then, he shifted his attention to the left-hand-side theme, the bomb explosion at the Olympics. He began the Olympic scene by drawing a sun in the top left-hand corner of the page. (This particular sun is not visible because it has been blocked out, for reasons illustrated in the following excerpt – the sun which *is* visible actually is a *third* sun that was added later.)

> C: Woopsies! I've done the sun at the wrong side.
>
> I: Did you? Where did you want to do it?
>
> C: Over here. (*Points to the right-hand side of the page.*)
>
> I: Over there. Oh, why's that?
>
> C: Because that's the other side of the world, and that's this side [Australia].
>
> I: Oh. Right. Well there's no taking it off now.
>
> C: Who cares. I'll just draw over it.

Ethan completes the rectangle to 'frame' the Olympic theme, and then fills out the left border of the frame with thicker, colouring-in lines which cover most of the sun. This line extends across the top of the page to connect with the sun on the right-hand side of the page – the line gradually tapers as the black fades into light, thus 'fading out' the left-hand theme and 'fading in' the right-hand theme. Later, after developing the right-hand theme, Ethan returns to the Olympic scene and turns it back into daytime by drawing a *third* sun, 'rising' on the other side of the world (see Figure 5.9).

> And now its sunny. *Squeezes the third sun in between the black scribble-out lines and the metal from the explosion.* The sun is shining up here where all the medals are. And it's dark over here at night time.

Ethan's ingenious use of the transitional device of fading out and fading in, to shift from daytime to night time and back to daytime again, allowed for the portrayal of parallel events within one drawing. The timing of the final fade in, where the third sun was inserted to 'light up' the Olympics again, occurred at the end of the Police Place sequence – to give this second theme closure. Ethan's repetition of the second fade-in device allowed for the potential development of yet another, new sequence. However, by this stage in the narrative, the 'story was over' – all that was to be told had been told. The final sun metaphorically functioned as a closing statement for the overall graphic-narrative-embodied play, something like, 'and another new day begins'.

In some ways, Ethan's parallel depiction of themes was like the film technique of *cross-cutting*. The events alternated, interweaved and interspersed one narrative action with another in different locations, thus combining the two. Parallel action took place simultaneously. The pioneer of parallel time story-telling in film, D.-W. Griffith, got the idea from Charles Dickens's technique of 'cutting' between parallel story lines in his novels (Rabiger, 2008, p. 186). Cross-cutting is often used to dramatically build tension and suspense in chase scenes, or to compare two different scenes, like in the film *The Godfather* (1972), where the baptism of Michael Corleone's godson is cross-cut with the violent elimination of Corleone's multiple underworld rivals. Although Ethan's parallel scenes were not as violent as that depicted in *The Godfather*, elements of tension and suspense were created through the thematic juxtaposition of chase scenes – athletes on one side of the world, and police dogs and criminals on the other side.

So let's look more closely at Ethan's content in this second theme (see Figure 5.10). Near the centre of the 'Police Place', Ethan draws a slide with a dog at the base, then a second dog at the top of the ladder, and a third dog gliding down the slide (the fourth dog shown in Figure 5.10 is actually part of another sequence, described later). These three dogs are actually one dog, illustrated in three different positions, similar to freeze frames in a film – a single image was repeated to give the illusion of a frozen action sequence. Like in cartoon animation, the repeated images depict the changing movement positions of the dog from one state to the next. The viewer of the drawing is to imagine the *in betweens* – the individual drawings that link the dog at the base of the ladder to the dog at the top, and between this dog and the one sliding down the slope. This dynamic event was intensified by Ethan's use of onomatopoeia, 'Whoops!' accompanied with a swooping gesture of his hand as the third dog slid down the slide. Together, the 'Whoops!' and the gesture *audiated-animated* the action sequence.

I: So that's the dogs training is it?

C: Yeah.

Figure 5.10   Dogs Running Over Slide [detail]

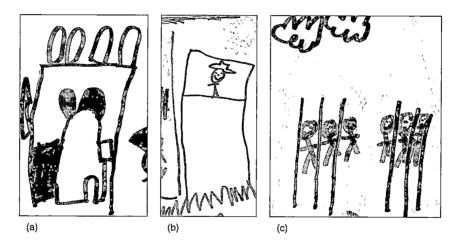

(a)   (b)   (c)

Figure 5.11   Frames for Theme-Based Sequences [details]

I: And they're training to ... what, run up the ladder are they?

C: Yeah, and go ... and run down it. That's when it's going up, and that's when it's up the top, and that's when it's going down.

I: OK so there's only really one dog here. It's just in different positions. OK.

To the left of the dog-training slide, Ethan draws a blue rectangular police car, shown from 'bird's eye view' (see Figure 5.11a) with red and blue lights on the top. To the right of the slide he draws a tall watch tower with a policeman standing guard (Figure 5.11b). Then, located at the top of the page, above the slide, he draws two house-shaped jails with two sets of three criminals inside (Figure 5.11c). These three

Figure 5.12   Policeman and Dog Chasing Criminal [detail]

frames serve as contextualizing devices within a composition of three scenes (ie a sequence) occurring in the Police Place.

As with the three dogs, Ethan repeats images to illustrate a sequence of actions – a policeman and a police dog capturing and jailing a 'bad person' (Figure 5.12). Ethan shifts the dog's role from running over the slide, to chasing the criminal. The criminal is shown twice, first escaping from jail and then being put back in jail. Ethan explains: 'This [scene] is where all the guard dogs are going after the person. Because he's the one that's escaping. But here they caught him and put him in jail'.

Later, at the bottom of the page, Ethan adds another scene in which he, as policeman, is depicted a second time, catching a pig, with the assistance of his police dog, 'TJ' (Figure 5.13). Ethan says, 'they're trying to catch the pig because it keeps on hurting people'.

Finally, Ethan illustrates another before-and-after event by repeating images to represent shifts in *time* and *space*. When asked what he will do in the future he describes moving to a different house, and shows his before-and-after houses in two locations. He draws a stylized house in the bottom right-hand corner of the page, with him standing beside it, saying, 'This is when I'm leaving home. And here's where I am ... where I'm living now' (he squeezes a new house into the available space next to the police car). Locating this 'future' house at the Police Place establishes Ethan's identity as a police officer when he grows up (Figure 5.14).

When asked if there was a story that goes with the drawing, Ethan presented a truncated version, which bore very little resemblance to the richness of characters, objects, scenes, events and dual-depiction of

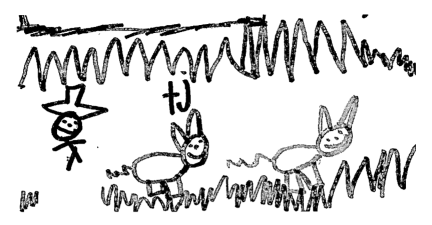

Figure 5.13   Ethan and TJ Chasing Pig [detail]

Figure 5.14   Leaving Home [detail]

world affairs that were drawn, told and enacted over 30 minutes. Ethan essentially 'fast forwarded' to the very last episode, skipping everything else that had led up to this. He simply reiterated this final segment, which fitted with the topic of drawing what the future may be like and, implicitly, what he would be doing: 'This is when I'm an adult, and I'm leaving home. And this is where I'm a ... when I'm bigger'.

This story is like the renditions that adults often hear when they ask children to tell them about their artworks after the event. Such synopses are not representative of the full graphic-narrative-embodied play event and do little justice to the depth of children's thinking and feeling that occurred *within* the visual narrative's *interpretive space* during the child's process of creation. Post-hoc story renditions do not contain the richness of content nor capture the *form* of participation that actually occurs during the child's enactment. If an adult does not witness the holistic event, which is filled with emotional undertones and connotations, his/her understanding of how the artwork functioned will be relatively superficial. In this case, the key concepts shown in Ethan's work – his turning the night into day, the dog running over the slide, and the criminal being chased and put back in jail – would be less vibrant, and particularly if re-told some time after the artwork was composed, the rendition likely would lose its freshness because it would be detached from role-played enactment and the real-time depiction with its associated emotions.

One needs to witness the 'live' representation to grasp the unfolding of signs within the overall shaping of the text. By watching the graphic depiction, listening to the narrative and noting the gestures and expressive vocalisms of the child, we come closer to understanding the holistic meaning-making act. This is a 'co-emergence' of content and form, and the child's work is a *composition in progress*, building layers of characterization, changing settings, frames of movement and integrated scenes.

A most striking example of this is shown in a final artwork of an 8-year-old boy, Jacob, which includes several, interconnected scenes within a complete and unified dramatic event. The drawing, entitled *Semi-Taxi and Sky Patrol*, is shown at the beginning of this chapter (Figure 5.1). It is an exceptional depiction of multiple sequences within a composition of scenes. The end of each is indicated by a change in time, action and location.

Multiple scenes in one work

Jacob's visual narrative presents like an *action film*, with parallel events (which often contain violence) taking place simultaneously. Chase scenes and conflicts between characters were used to dramatically build tension and suspense within and across scenes. Action-packed qualities imply that *everything, everywhere* is occurring *simultaneously* – indeed, at a frantic pace. Jacob's narrative interweaves one scene with another, in different locations, combining these in a parallel fashion.

The ambiance of the drawing is visually 'live' – a quality that is achieved by the artist's use of numerous *action lines* to show movement. The scenery metaphorically screeches with movement, like a *tracking shot* in film, where the camera moves alongside the action (on a dolly or truck), 'tracking within' the visual space. If one were to imagine the sound-track that might accompany the artwork, it would likely be similar to that of a *James Bond* film.

However, compared to the visual vibrancy of the artwork, Jacob's narrative is matter of fact and impartial. As an *omniscient narrator*, Jacob describes characters and events, even those which include vio-lence, in a distant third-person voice, as if he is standing outside the action. His connotative meaning, which centres on themes of safety, surveillance and law enforcement, is depicted in a *prototypical* way. Yet the content suggests a real connectedness with all characters and events, as if Jacob is 'being' everyone, 'doing' everything.

Jacob begins his work by describing a semi-trailer taxi which can transport cars down the freeway when the drivers feel they need a rest. A complete transcription of Jacob's telling is provided, to illustrate how the scenes unfolded in a non-linear but integrated fashion. This begins with Jacob drawing a base line about a third of the way from the bot-tom of the page and a semi-trailer, with a driver in the cabin, and three cars suspended by hooks from the top of the semi-trailer.

I: Here's a big semi, is it?

C: Yeah. And some carrying cars, in case you're tired ... you just get hooked up by it and have a rest.

I: I see. I can see the big hooks there.

C: Yeah, they carry the cars and when you need a rest, you just can go to sleep, and that travels wherever you want it to go. It's like a taxi carrying lots of cars. *Adds two cars entering the back of the semi-trailer, moving up a ramp. Adds whoosh lines to show the movement of the cars. Adds speech balloons to the people in the suspended cars, with the letters ZZZ to show that they are sleeping.*

I: They have numbers on them, do they? Oh ... no they're not num-bers. They're ... snoring, are they? Oh *(laughs)*, they're the people in there snoring. Right, so they're resting. So, sort of, can you drive on there while it's going along, can you?

C: Yeah. You just drive up, and then you get hooked up ... onto it, and then it drives wherever you want. *Draws a large sun in the top left-hand corner, with several different coloured sections.*

I: What are you doing now? Oh, that's the Sun is it?

C: Mmmm. It's a *future* sun.

I: OK. How is the future sun different to the sun now?

C: *Adds another car entering the truck.* Mmm. 'Cause ... oh ... it's not really just yellow that's shining from the sun. It's like ... pink ... and green ... and the sun is sort of like different colours. The sun itself ... is blue and yellow, lots of different colours. It's volumed by someone ... um, it's volumed by the person in the semi-trailer ... how hot it goes and how cold it goes.

I: Mmm. So ... what? That person can control the sun, can they? How do they do that?

C: Well, [with] a special sort of like remote control. *Draws a purple zigzag line ascending from the cab of the semi-trailer going up to the sun, with a splash line to show that it has made contact.*

I: So they can control the heat?

C: Yeah, and the coldness. So ... there's light blue and dark blue in there. And um they can take out the ... sort of like...hot colours, like red and yellow. And they can leave in sort of like the cold colours, like blue and green. *Draws a red zigzag line descending from the sun, with a splash line where it reaches the cab of the semi-trailer.*

I: Alright. Is that sort of the remote control there is it?

C: Yeah, that's the um thing that's getting ... he's making it a bit colder. *Adds wavy lines below the cab to show warming/cooling of the semi-trailer. Draws a two-cab helicopter above the semi-trailer with hover lines below it.*

I: Now what's this up in the sky?

C: It's sort of like a two-people helicopter. It's got one person at the back. It can go backwards with that person. It can go frontwards with that person. *Adds dots above the rotor blades. Draws a brown aerial on top of the semi-trailer and a zigzag line to connect the aerial with the helicopter.* An aerial.

I: And what does that connect it to? What/who can they sort of contact?

C: They can listen to the radio, and they can contact um the helicopter and that rocket. *Draws a sky patrol in the top right-hand section.*

I: Is that a rocket is it over there? Mmm hmm. What does that do?

C: Oh, it's just sort of like a sky patrol.

I: Oh, right ... so it's patrolling the sky at all times is it?

C: Yep. Like if any plane's like ... tryin' to land other aircrafts, that sky patrol can just come along and just hook 'em with a hook. I'm just going to draw a funny type of plane trying to ram a helicopter.

I: So there's a sky patrol ...

C: Yeah, and he's on duty, because someone's trying to ram that helicopter. *Adds a small brown antennae on top of each of the cars in the semi-trailer.*

I: Are they sort of like the police, the sky patrol?

C: Yeah. *Draws a plane behind the helicopter.*

I: Do the sky patrol have any sort of thing to do with the people in the cars and that?

C: Yeah, in case there's a car crash, or something like that ... they just land somewhere near it. And if there are any injured people, they just get out their stretcher and take them back to the hospital. So they're a bit like on-the-ground police and off-the-ground police. *Adds 'ramming lines' in front of the plane.*

I: So what's this other plane? This is the naughty one is it, that's going to ram the ah ... looks like he *has* rammed him.

C: Yeah. *Adds blue 'radar' dots to the sky patrol and labels the jet.*

I: And so then what does the sky patrol do?

C: Oh, he has ... *draws a large hook between the sky patrol and the plane.*

I: Sends out a hook or something, does he?

C: Yeah, it sort of like ... it stops them from going any further.

I: Mmm hmm. And what would they do with them then, when they got ...

C: Oh, they probably just take them back to the sky patrol station.

I: Mmm hmm ... and what would they do to them?

C: Oh, probably give them a fine, or take them to jail or court. Or they could just take the person out who rammed them ... and um just put them in jail.

I: *(laughs)*

C: And they have a little, sort of like sucking thing that, like, sucks on to the back of their engine so they can't move any further. *Adds a suction hook to the sky patrol, connecting to the back of the plane, with suction lines inside it.* The hook is on the front one, but the suction thing is on the back.

I: Mmm. So he certainly wouldn't get away, with all that, would he ... with the suction and the hook...?

C: Nuh. *Adds a radar disc on top of the semi-trailer with a zigzag line ascending to the back of the sky patrol.* I made a little radar on the semi-trailer. It's a sort of square with a, sort of like, cake piece out of it ... that detects like all hot things, like fire and the sun (*gestures with pen – circular movements in the air*). And like it detects all the engines. And sometimes when it hits the engines, the sky planes could go down. *Adds whoosh lines to the opening back door of the semi-trailer and small whoosh lines behind the front and back wheels of the semi-trailer. Adds a grid to the front of the cab, with exhaust coming from it and an exhaust chimney on top of the semi-trailer with a cloud coming from this. Adds numbers to each car inside the semi-trailer.*

I: Is that all the smoke and pollution coming out of the truck, is it?

C: Yeah. They use up a lot of fuel.

I: Does this truck, um, go continuously, does it?

C: Yeah. It ... oh ... whatever country it's in, it takes about, it takes the first person to get on it and then say, the first person gets on and says, 'Oh I want to go to, say, Perth' and it'll get over there in 10 minutes. And the second person gets on 'I want to go to Mackay'. But the first person that gets on gets the first trip, and then the second person gets the second trip, the last person has to wait quite a while to get where they want to go.

I: Mmm. What if you get sick of being on there, can you get off?

C: Oh, yeah, you can easily just get off, because um like, there's another wheel there, and there's a tunnel through, between the wheels just there. *Adds tunnel below the back of the cab.* And the hooks just lower you down. *Adds an extended hook with a car being lowered.* And then you just drive beside it, like overtaking it ... or you could just drive backwards, through the tunnel *(gestures to demonstrate).*

I: Mmm. So what's the idea of the numbers on the car there?

C: Oh ... like ... so police can detect them. Like they have special numbers on them, and ... say, if the first one had number five, no other car could have number five on it ... unless it's in another country. And no other country cars are allowed to come in to one of these [semi-taxis]. *(Uses pen in hand to gesture just above the drawing to illustrate his description.)*

I: So they all have numbers on them. That helps the police check on them, does it?

C: Yeah, so they've checked all the people out.

I: How do people feel about that ... having a number on their car, and the police knowing who they are, and all that?

C: Well, I mean, they don't really have much choice, because they have to. It's like 'Have one on there'. It's the, oh, government's or police's choice ... to have numbers on the cars ... so that the police can detect them. The people in the cars with the numbers on ... if they do a crime, and someone saw the number on the car, they'd just be detected. And they'd just go to court and say if they did it. Well ... there is another problem with it though. Someone could easily just sort of like hop into that number five car, and the other person would hop into their car, and their car was number seven, and the person in that car would get the blame for it.

I: Yeah. So in one way it's helpful, and in another way it's ... er ...

C: Reduces crime. *Adds a small dot to each of the antennas in the cars in the semi-trailer. Draws a caravan inside the semi-trailer, with a driver in front and exhaust coming out from three points of the caravan.*

I: What's that you've drawn inside the truck now?

C: Oh, that's a new design car. It goes a bit faster, but except it makes more pollution. Sort of like a caravan car that people can sleep in, in case they get tired when they're going on a trip. They think 'Oh man, I don't want to sleep outside'. They can just sleep in their sort of like little house. It comes with a sink and a bathroom and a bed. And all of the big caravan cars, their numbers have gotta be at least a hundred, or over a hundred. And if they like have decoration like I'm doing to this caravan car *(adds decorations and the number 100 to the caravan)*, it cannot be, um, touching the number ... otherwise the police can't detect it.

I: Mmm hmm, so it has to be clearly visible.

C: Yep, to the police up in the air. It either has a little arrow, *adds arrow,* or it sort of like glows in the dark. *Draws truck in front of the semi-trailer, standing on its end. Adds brown wavy lines across the bottom of the page.*

C: This is dirt, and in the dirt they have sort of like ... um ... underground cameras. So the underground cameras are all along. *Adds a camera to the dirt.* Like, the big semi-trailer that carries the trucks ... it goes only certain places. So the people know what certain places it goes, because they get a little booklet when they enter the town. And all along the roads where it goes, there's these little cameras under it. *Adds second camera in the dirt.* Because the other cars that are coming toward don't know there's cameras. In case like, one of the car drivers they think ... oh ... they might take over driving ... like, sort of like murder the person that's trying to take them where they want, because it like, can't get there that fast. They've got these little cameras under all the roads where it travels, so if any criminal or person that he doesn't know, that he probably thinks is not good, if he tries to bash him up, the cameras will just beep real real loud, and they'll just give a signal to the sky patrol, so that the sky patrol can sort of hear them.

I: Well there's certainly a lot of controls on people, isn't there?

C: Yeah. 'Cause they don't want any crimes in the city or on the roads.

I: Right. So all of this is in an effort ...

C: Yeah, from the council ... or whoever made it.

I: Does it seem to work?

C: Well ... it has worked the most times they've used it but, it might have a fault in it ... so if there's a fault in it, the criminals could just get away, get away with it. *Adds two cameras on the ceiling of the trailer of the semi-trailer.* Here's a ... there's a sort of like camera just in the corner of the back ... to detect all the cars ... that there's no sort of like guns in there.

I: Right. Golly there's so many things in this picture ... what am I up to? I don't think you told me about that car on its side there in front of the truck.

C: Oh yeah. *Adds two cameras in the dirt.* Um it's sort of a ... like ... it can go, sort of like, on its back. And if it wants to go a bit faster, it just flips back onto its normal wheels.

I: Wow. Look at all that technology. So this is the future. Are you in the picture anywhere? What do you think *you* might be doing, if you are in the picture?

C: Might have been driving the semi-trailer, or the sky patrol. I want to be a pilot when I grow up because my dad is.

I: Would you be able to give your picture a name?

C: Um ... The Future? (*Writes 'The Future' at the top of the page.*)

I: And why did you call it that?

C: Because ... it is the future.

I: OK. About how old are you in the picture? Say, perhaps if you're the sky patrol pilot?

C: Um ... 24? (*Taps the Sky Patrol and smiles.*)

Jacob used a number of graphic devices to show movement:

- *hover lines* below the double-direction helicopter,
- *ramming lines* in front of the plane as it hits the back of the helicopter,
- *flames* at the back of the sky patrol,
- *exhaust puffs* from the back, front or top of the various ground vehicles,
- *zigzag lines* to make radar 'visible',
- *splash lines* to show 'contact' with the sun and the cab of the semi-trailer,
- *whoosh lines* to denote movement of cars and the opening of the back door of the semi-trailer, and
- *suction lines* to indicate that the sky patrol had connected with the back of the airplane.

These helped support his action-based sequence. Hooking and un-hooking themes served as a unifying device, lending a plot thread to two *scenes* within his visual narrative:

(a) cars hooking to the top of the semi-taxi and unhooking when they want to leave, and
(b) the sky patrol hooking and sucking on to the back of the aircraft to prevent it from ramming the helicopter.

Hooking and un-hooking *archetypically* connoted a *plot* content which centred on two issues:

(a) liberating – releasing drivers from fatigue and letting them go when they had recovered, and
(b) capturing – preventing crime and taking the offenders back to the sky patrol station.

These issues were embedded in several scientific *concepts*, including:

(a) radar – to allow for human communication through the dish on top of the semi-taxi and aerials on top of the semi-taxi and the cars inside it and on the sky patrol,
(b) heat detection – to note the actions of the sky patrol and other ground or air vehicles, and
(c) temperature – to provide comfort for the passengers in the semi-taxi.

Controllable solar energy allowed the driver of the semi-taxi to par-tial out colours from the sun to heat or cool the cab. The artist's choice of colours was *metaphoric*: 'bright' colours (e.g., red, orange, yellow) stood for *warm*, and 'dark' colours (e.g., blue, purple, black) stood for *cool*. Jacob also used metaphor to describe how the sun was 'powered' by the semi-trailer taxi driver, who could 'volume' the temperature.

  The two main themes of (a) safety and (b) surveillance/law enforcement punctuated and sustained the action-packed drama involving several machines speeding through space, where skir-mishes were enacted and violence (e.g., bashing the driver) and issues of theft were real possibilities. The characters in the various ground vehicles and aircrafts all had *roles* to play in this episodic adventure:

- the *car drivers* were entering or exiting the semi-taxi, having a snooze in between,
- the *semi-taxi driver* was not only driving, but also controlling the tem-perature through the use of a remote control, while simultaneously

monitoring, through the surveillance cameras, the behaviour of the vehicle owners in the back of the truck, and

• the *sky patrol pilot* was preventing the aggressive collision of the airplane and the helicopter, while communicating with back-at-base police about bringing the aircraft down and capturing the pilot to take him to jail.

These roles and associated events would not have been vivid without the inclusion of the action lines. The whoosh and zigzag lines and dots (i.e., aerial transmission to cars) connoted interactions and anchored the sequences, providing *inter-connectivity* between the characters and their actions. These devices provided evidence of the embodied nature of Jacob's involvement while layering the *multilinear* structure of the artwork.

Jacob's fluid unfolding of 'radiational' thoughts and feelings frequently involved explaining the meaning of what he had just drawn while simultaneously drawing a new idea or adding graphic devices to some component of the work, to clarify movements and provide conceptual links. He regularly returned to previous images to elaborate ideas through visual detail, and extended the themes accordingly. This revisiting of ideas provided opportunities for Jacob to build the plot thread and to add coherence between plot points – an essential component of any good storyline. The compositional development was an ongoing process of *revision*.

Jacob's *thought-in-action episodes*, which centred on characters and events, shifted in and out of an overall framework, where the complete structure evolved in bits and pieces, unified by 'big picture' concepts of safety and law enforcement. The result was similar to what the film-maker Jean-Luc Godard declared he liked about a film – 'it should have a beginning, a middle and an end, but not necessarily in that order' (cited in Chandler, 2002, p. 90). Jacob's unfolding plot was play-like, spontaneous and free-form as he took on multiple roles and shaped the characters' actions and associated scenery at will. The evolution was reminiscent of a scene from one of the *Indiana Jones* movies, when after a series of fabulistic events which have led to a fever-pitched state of affairs, the female lead panics as she sees Indi mounting a horse, about to race away and leave her to fend for herself. She shouts, 'Where are you going *now*?' Indi replies, 'I don't know, I'm making this up as I go'. Such is the nature of graphic-narrative-embodied play – it evolves in relation to what the imagination suggests.

Summary

Children's fabulistic stories seem to be generated from a combination of personal experience and imagination with *intertextual* undertones. These creative encounters provide textual spaces in which children can plan, enact and examine worlds from the inside. Children play and replay imaginary worlds, making a range of authorial choices involving visual action, character development, plot and scenery. Such processes empower children to make choices about coherence and disruption (Dyson, 1997; Sutton-Smith, 1995), about power and powerlessness and about a range of other issues.

Even though the creator of *The Olympics and the Police Place* labelled himself and the dog in his drawing, it was reasonably clear that the message was meant to be prototypic rather than specific. It connoted defending-capturing through figures that had broad-ranging, 'standing for' functions. Ethan's schema of a single dog represented all of the dogs at the Police Place: 'and this is where all the guard dogs are going after the person', implying a representative set of dogs, in the wings, so to speak – on standby for that scene.

Such prototypicality is suggested in the titles of the artists' works and their reluctance to constitute their allegorical narratives in a 'story' format. Jacob's words, 'It is the future', imply that what had just been witnessed was a *fabulistic reality in the making*. Similarly, Ethan seemed so ensconced in other-worldliness that, when asked if there was a story to accompany his work, he seemed to be jolted back into the grown-up's mind frame. His truncated version simply repeated the mundane finale of him leaving home, complying with the traditional story format of an 'ending' stemming from a 'beginning'. Yet all of the 'middle' – the meat of the artwork – would have been lost without the documentation of the complete graphic-narrative-embodied event.

Such play-based works are short-lived, poetic and free-form. They are fleeting encounters, rendered visible when we enter children's fantasy worlds and really listen to all that is communicated – visually, verbally and physically. Children's fundamental drive to make meaning can be powerfully captured in their amorphous, otherworldly visual narratives. The dialogue of graphic-narrative-embodied play integrates 'what the eye sees, the mind constructs, and the hand creates' (Golomb, 2004, p. 191). Like in the dominant genre of films and novels, art plays a part in the constitution of the self, providing a safe space in which children can create and shape their worlds at will, imaginatively.

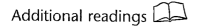 Reflections

1. Revisit the artworks of children that you have collected and describe these in relation to *syntopic, synchronic, diatopic* and *diachronic* features. If there was more than one event in a child's drawing, develop a *storyboard* to depict these events.
2. Share these storyboards with your classmates and analyse the *stills, scenes* or *sequences* in relation to the structure of the child's visual narrative.
3. What verbal, gestural and graphic cues were used to imply a *shift of scenes* between *plot points* in children's artworks?
4. What themes and concepts were *denoted* and *connoted* in the children's works?

Additional readings 📖

Dyson, A.H. (1997). *Writing superheroes: Contemporary childhood, popular culture, and classroom literacy.* New York: Teachers College Press.

Kline, S. (1993). *Out of the garden: Toys, TV, and children's culture in the age of marketing.* London: Verso.

Sutton-Smith, B. (1995). Play as performance, rhetoric, and metaphor. *Play and Culture, 2,* 189–192.

Ancient Forms → New Worlds

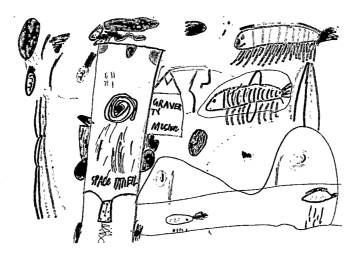

Figure 6.1   New Planet in 5000 (boy, 8.5)

At the completion of this chapter, you should be able to:

1. Understand how dualisms are a child's first logical operation, which help children categorize and generate order out of complex human experience,
2. Describe how binary concepts, such as good and evil, are applied in children's thinking within their visual narratives, and
3. Reflect on how ancient forms (e.g. allegory) and contemporary forms (e.g. film) are used as inspirations for young children's visual narratives.

The signs that children use to communicate their imaginary worlds often contain underlying ideologies. In the artwork above (Figure 6.1), the boy (8.5) explores supernatural concepts, set within the context of a 'newly discovered' planet in the year 5000. The artist establishes spatial relationships by locating Earth toward the centre of the page, saying 'Earth is *aaaaaall* the way back here'. He positions the moon below and right of Earth and adds Saturn in the top left-hand corner of the page. His plot, which evolves from the features of science fiction, includes:

- *characters* (e.g., humans and aliens, with one alien featured with a jetpack flying above the high rise building),
- *settings* (e.g., a building with weights 'so that gravity doesn't pull it right up' and a gravity machine which pumps gravity into the building so that people 'don't have to fly around'), and
- *objects and events* (e.g., the Fish Spaceship's force field tapping into the building's gravity machine, and two hover cars having an accident).[1]

This artist, like many other children whose work is presented in this chapter, understood that a plot which carries moral implications is interesting; an awareness likely picked up from media such as film, theatre, novels and oral story-telling traditions. He embraced good plot-development techniques by establishing subtexts, where characters' values were illustrated in their behaviours and through tensions between their inner and outer worlds – between what the characters wanted and what impeded them from acting on something.

For instance, when drawing the alien grub ship (top right-hand corner) the boy explains that the aliens inside are grubs and 'are kind of like the people who stop robbers. They are police, like the FBI, but only do alien work'. He elaborates that this spaceship is:

> powered by some sort of thing from humans, either fear, scared or surprise. And they keep humans onboard and make them scared, so they mostly do it surprise. So they surprise them and all of those things help control it. And right now they are on a case and chasing a police alien, but [he's] a smuggler [of] drugs. He is pretending he is a policeman, but he has forgotten that policemen can go to jail for drug smuggling. They've got 50 humans on board the ship and are making them surprised. They are so good they are going faster and can catch up.

---

[1] For more details about this drawing-telling, see Wright (2005, 2007a, b).

Further tension between characters is expressed in association with the 'mind lines' (the parallel rainbow-coloured lines 'shining down' on the left-hand side of the page). He explains that these:

> stop people from going across to another dimension. They give people electric shocks like static shocks, like when you rub your feet against carpet and then they touch people like them. And some people like that getting done, so they keep trying to get past. But they don't know if the aliens over there might kill them. The man who mutated into an alien knows what's past there but not the other aliens.

This force field (to prevent humans from 'going across') and the alien FBI's use of human psychic energy (to speed up the spaceship) are imaginative devices to create metaphysical tensions and impediments. The artist surfaces the deeper ideologies of the characters through fantasy-based thinking inspired by popular media. Like a fiction film or a short story, which are consumed in a single sitting, the child's visual narrative continues the tradition of oral story-telling.

In former times, oral story-telling constituted, along with religion, most of the common person's education. Today, the cinema's pre-eminence has overtaken oral story-telling traditions, and similarly provides unparalleled power to make us see and feel from another's point of view. As Rabiger (2008) explains, through the screen:

> we can temporarily become braver, funnier, stronger, angrier, more beautiful, more vulnerable, or more beset with danger and tragedy. A good movie sends us out energized and refreshed in spirit. This cathartic contact with the trials of the human spirit is a need as fundamental as eating [and] breathing ... Art, of which the cinema is but the youngest form, nourishes our spirit by engaging us in surrogate emotional experience and implying underlying patterns. (p. 175)

Developing themes from the previous chapter, I aim to illustrate how popular media draws upon traditional forms of myth and allegory through the interplay between binary oppositions, such as good/ evil, dominance/submission, real/imaginary or natural/ supernatural. Children utilize such themes in their creation of visual narratives. But such binary concepts do not only make for a gripping story: they have a deeper, more fundamental role to play in children's cognition and moral development. They offer a way for young children to 'spontaneously make sense of the world and experience' (Egan, 1999, p. 33). Indeed, for young children, dualism is a child's first logical operation; it is a function of the structure of the human mind (Lévi-Strauss, 1966).

Binaries and thought

Binaries help us categorize and generate order out of complex human experience (Jakobson & Halle, 1956) and 'provide a basic marker of humanity' (Leach, 1982, p. 109). The oppositions universally found in the representational traditions of societies around the world include: good/evil, self/other, subject/object, masculine/feminine, light/dark, body/mind, positive/negative, nature/history, sacred/profane, heaven/hell (Danesi, 2007). Claude Lévi-Strauss's analysis of myths identified similar sets of binary opposites, which he claimed were constructs used to demonstrate a kind of logic in the tangible qualities of phenomena of everyday life, 'of the raw and the cooked, honey and ashes, and so on' (Lévi-Strauss, 1969, p. 1).

Through early discrimination between hot and cold, for instance, children come to grasp mediating concepts such as warm. On a more imaginative plane, when children draw, they are free to use mediating concepts to depict creatures such as ghosts (which are both alive and dead), aliens (which are both human and other) and natural creatures that use language, wear clothes and have emotions (Egan, 1999). This is a fascinating feature of children's thinking, which accounts for their easy engagement with both fantasy and exotic real-life content. Egan urges that, while children's classifications may seem unsophisticated, we should endeavour to understand the logic that they are using in forming these.

The artwork above provides evidence of early abstract thought and a 'personalization of theory' (Goody, 1977, p. 42). This was shown through the artist's synaesthetic description of the humans onboard being given 'fear or surprise' to 'power' the spaceship, and humans' persistence in trying to get through the mind lines, in spite of the immense electric shocks they receive. Although he did not use abstract terms explicitly, his concepts of psychic energy and force fields were tied to *affective abstraction*. Similar abstractions, described in the previous chapter, included dualistic interplays between good and evil and capturing and defending. These also were reflected in the *plot threads* of Ethan's and Jacob's narratives (presented in Chapter Five) in the following ways:

- Ethan drew a policeman and police dog chasing a criminal to put him back in jail and athletes competing at an Olympic event, which was jeopardized by a bomb explosion. He also contrasted light with dark, a common binary opposition used in ancient mythology. However in Ethan's visual narrative, the light–dark juxtaposition

Figure 6.2   Dual Parks and Pollution (boy, 8.1)

did not include a good side of the world versus an evil side. Instead, both sides of the world contained both good and evil,
- Jacob's cameras and radar linked to all vehicles served a surveillance function in crime prevention. Symbols and icons were used to communicate how licence plate numbers, radar lines, and aerials and antennae were used to monitor people's behaviour.

For thousands of years, similar themes of good/evil and other binaries were reflected in the myths, legends, folklore and fairytales that were passed down from generation to generation. These resources were used to impart sublime truths accessible in no other way (Campbell, 1991). Today, the features of the texts of popular media, such as *Harry Potter* and *Lord of the Rings*, continue to be based on 'powerful conflicts between security and danger, courage and cowardice, cleverness and stupidity, hope and despair, and good and evil' (Bettelheim, 1976, p. 74).

Similarly, in the event-based artwork shown in Figure 6.2, a powerful juxtaposition of healthy–sick and preservation–destruction is illustrated by a boy (8.1) who contrasts two parks, one living and one dying, to depict concepts of pollution. He sets the context by explaining the scenery of the work:

This car will be a lot faster. There'll be a lot more flames coming out of the back. Smoke. And the airplane will fly a lot farther than we do [now] and get the people and luggage across a lot faster, from the airports to across the sea. It's got a lot of smoke coming out the back, joining up with the car, and that makes it more smoke.

The artist describes the causes of pollution and its affect on animals, people and the environment, and how people's greed and lack of government policies have failed to address these concerns.

There'll be lots of cars, trucks and motorcycles ... noise pollution. And a lot of our seas won't be as nice as they are now. Because ... of ... us ... because whenever we get more buildings, we start not caring about what we already had. 'Cause all the smoke would cause a lot of acid rain – it's rain with a lot of pollution and stuff in it ... and chemicals. And these are electricity centres. And that's all the smoke coming out.

These are trees from a far distance. And these little things are birds flying around. And a waterfall. I'm going to put a sign there to say that they're going to be gone. And that's going to be the other waterfall, and I'm going to draw some dead trees.

We're not looking after it. And it's mainly our fault, not the animals'. Humans have been cutting down trees, and um ... looting ... taking other people's treasures, 'cause they've worked hard all their life to keep the parks a long time. They wanted that [non-polluted park] ... but the government didn't listen ... and, now it's that [polluted park]. There's a dead bird over here.

It won't be a nice place to live, if this did happen. There's two people walking here [healthy park]. But there's none here [dead park]. Because they wouldn't want to go here. On this side, they'd come back, but over here, that bird's kicking out now that it's nest's gone. It can't survive over here, 'cause some of the trees here are getting cut down. There is a lot of air pollution, noise pollution and [water] pollution that is making us feel not that good about ourselves.

Although this example is rooted in current affairs, children often push beyond the boundaries of realism though visual narratives that are more closely aligned with mythology. In such cases, dialectical worlds are animated through tensions, which are organized around moral imperatives, such as right and wrong. Ancient myths provide the subtexts and intertexts of these plots, similar to how they are used in popular media today, like in the films *Superman*, *Star Wars* and *Star Trek*. As Rabiger (2008, p. 177) points out, 'under the guise of futurism' such films are 'really traditional morality plays'. Danesi's (2007) description below helps clarify how myths are:

a fundamental form of sense making in which the characters are 'gods, heroes, and mystical beings; the plots are about heroes, the origins of things, or meaningful human experiences; the settings involve metaphysical worlds juxtaposed against the real world; and the narrator is an unknown being from beyond the human sphere. Myths constitute metaphysical knowledge texts for explaining human origins and actions. (p. 108)

Pop culture heroes, like Superman, are adapted from ancient myths and legends. They often have great courage, strength and bravery and are celebrated for their boldness and generosity and their upholding of human ideals, such as honesty and justice. 'Like their ancestors, modern-day people need heroes subconsciously to "make things right" in human affairs, at least in the realm of the imagination' (Danesi, 2007, p. 125). This propensity to imaginatively depict heroes through visual narratives is evident in many examples of children's visual narratives. In the artwork at the beginning of this chapter (Figure 6.1), for instance, the alien at the top of the page has a jetpack which doubles as a parachute, and the effect presents as being visually reminiscent of Superman's cape (although the plot of the narrative illustrates that this character also has a 'bad' side).

In contemporary mass culture, we also encounter many events and ritualized spectacles that have a mythic origin. Danesi (2007) provides an excellent example of how football games, and the ritualized events leading up to and occurring at the game, represent heroes and opponents. Such constructs were presented in Chapter 4 in the 8-year-old boy's drawing of three Olympic athletes at the award ceremony (Figure 4.12). All three athletes are heroes, but the Australian is represented as better, compared to his Canadian and British opponents. The implicit audience is participating in the fanfare of the award ceremony, viewing the raising of the three flags and hearing the Australian national anthem. The tiered podium, the athletes' uniforms and the gold, silver and bronze medals are reminiscent of symbolism of mythical origin. Barthes distinguished between original myths and rituals and their modern-day versions in his book *Mythologies* (1957/1973), and how these are guided by features (e.g., settings, characters, events) that define their style and form (Danesi, 2007, p. 127).

When children work within a mythical plane, the 'rules of the universe' are metaphysical. The plot acts as a frame in which children enact their sense of life's causes and effects, but with imaginative dabs of fanciful ideas. Children can associate with the confidence, ingenuity, strength or whatever of their heroic characters and can transcend their constraints, arising triumphantly.

To illustrate this issue in relation to victories–defeats, the visual narratives of Ethan and Jacob introduced *complications* to tighten the tension, generate anticipation and create suspense. Complications were set up by an *antagonist*, such as the plane 'trying to land other aircrafts' or the criminal 'trying to escape from the Police Place'. The artists *built the scene*, bringing it to a climax, and then set the context for a shift to a new scene. These scenes functioned in a similar way to *acts* within a film or a play, divided by *plot points* – places of dramatic change. Shifts between plot points were foretold in the artists' narrative, through phrases such as 'this is where x happened' or 'if x, then y':

- Ethan: 'This is it, the Olympics, and that's where the bomb came', '[This is where] they're trying to catch the pig because it keeps on hurting people'
- Jacob: 'And if any plane's trying to land other aircrafts ... ', 'I made a little radar on the semi-trailer that detects the engines ...'.

An effective artwork, like a good film, can lead children to experience new conditions to expand their minds and hearts. Children, like adults, have a desire to experience, if only temporarily, the world of others. This is why drawing is so powerful. Young artists can project into the characters' predicaments, and multiple perspectives arise because 'each character sees differently' (Rabiger, 2008, p. 178).

Like mythical stories, children's visual narratives may contain dominant characters triumphing over evil, often armed with technological tools. Such narratives have been traced back to 19th-century action-adventure stories for children, and probably have existed in other forms for thousands of years. Today, elements of such stories can be found in comics, cartoons and contemporary children's films (Kline, 1993). For instance, the film *Shark Tale* (2004) is centred on a vegetarian shark anti-hero, who assists a scrawny little fish to stage a false shark attack. The outcome is that the little fish becomes constituted as a heroic shark slayer who saves his community.

Palmer (1986) and Sutton-Smith (1995) have discussed how young children seem to be drawn to stories that tap into such universal themes, which are deeply embedded in children's folk culture. Much of this folk culture is similar to allegory – a structure found in many forms of popular media, such as *Harry Potter*.

Allegory

The issues in allegory (e.g., bravery, security, safety and justice) are depicted through characters, figures and events in narrative and pictorial form, some of which include dramatization (http://dictionary. reference.com/browse/allegory). Allegory involves making suggestive

Figure 6.3   Magic Birds and Special Animals (boy, 6.3)

resemblances between a visible event or character and another, more abstract, level of meaning. 'Allegory and parable (from *parabola*, meaning curved plane or comparison) can hit a nerve in audiences very powerfully' (Rabiger, 2008, p. 189). For instance, the allegoric film *The Matrix* (1999) depicts a 'real' world that is actually a 'virtual' world, in which machines take over by using humans as a source of energy. Humans are kept in a state of 'dreaming the real world'. People from the world behind enter this metaphysical dimension, and some from the real world escape and fight against the machines. But this fight extends into the dream world, where the laws of physics become suspended, and where characters have supernatural abilities, such as being able to stop bullets mid flight.

Similarly, children's use of quasi-human figures offer them opportunities to polarize between real and fantasy worlds. As Paley demonstrates (1981, 1984, 1990), children's narratives move between fantasy and the exotic very rapidly, often through metaphorical leaps. Egan (1999) also points out that 'young children have no difficulty being engaged by the weirdest creatures in the most exotic locales' (Egan, 1999, p. 41). He adds that, for young children, magic is 'entirely unobjectionable as long as it moves the story along' (p. 45). An example, of magic, was drawn by a boy (6.3) whose content includes 'special' birds and animals, linked to his understanding of Santa and Jesus (Figure 6.3).

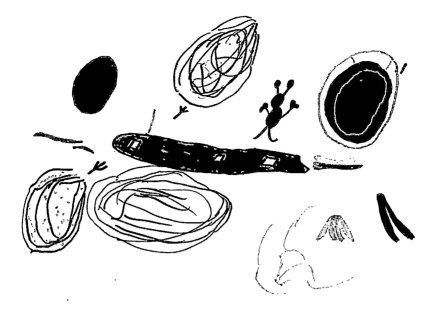

Figure 6.4   Family in Spaceship (girl, 6.2)

> They're magic birds ... they're special birds ... they help Santa. And they're special animals ... the wombat, the porcupine and the goanna ... they help Jesus because they're special.

Quasi-human figures were also used in the girl's (6.2) character-based artwork shown in Figure 6.4, which features a prototypic spaceship that she and her family use to travel to various planets. The people onboard, what they do in the spaceship and the type of resources they have reflect her personal life.

> This is the space ship, and the yellow bits are the lights on inside. And there's a little stick so you can drive it, with little um circles on top of it.

> The people inside are some of my cousins, and myself and my sister, and my Mum and Dad. Inside the spaceship there's some chairs with a little table and a little cupboard, where all the medicines are, if you get a little sick. And there's a little bedroom in there. And there's another big bedroom. And there's a sink. And a toilet. And there's um ... there's some toilet paper. And some toys. And there's a rocking chair – I've got a aunty in there too.

> I visit all the planets with my whole family. On Pluto, I just walk around the street and I leave the spaceship outside where the planets all are. My favourite planet is Pluto, 'cause it's got more people in it. I visit there to see who are there ... to see if who I know is there. Some are Japanese. And some are from Africa. Some are from England. And some are from Australia, and overseas. And that's about it. Oh, and an alien [the figure hovering above the spaceship].

Figure 6.5   Beyond 2050 (boy, 6.6)

The artist's description of the alien introduces plot tension. However, rather than combating the alien, the girl prefers to avoid conflict by staying 'out of sight'. This is described in relation to an unfolding family theme and two baby aliens (fork-shaped figures, below and above the spaceship). She incorporates classic fairytale characters of a king and queen into her narrative, who are also aliens.

> Um, that's little aliens. This little alien is trying to get through to the other alien, 'cause they're babies. The big alien is fierce. And he talks nasty to people in other planets, and he's got all his friends, and they're all fierce too. He's got a little baby boy, it's nice. And they don't be fierce to him, the alien, the big fierce one. And there's a king and a queen. Um there's one that's fierce. The king's fierce. I mean the queen's fierce, and the king's not. When I see them, they don't see me because I go to another planet. If all the aliens are at um Pluto, and then I go out of there; they come back to Spotty Planet, and I go back to Pluto.

Although this artwork included fantasy and quasi-human figures, the content was more *character-based* than event-based. Even the avoidance of the nasty aliens was centred predominantly on her travelling to other planets to meet up with friends who might happen to be there. By contrast, the work in Figure 6.5 centres on *events* involving sci-fi *technology*, including a car that can fly (bottom, centre of page). John (6.6) imaginatively applies concepts of solar and fuel-based power, gravity and day–night relationships in various parts of the world.

Okay, I'm just going to draw the family car first, with special air bubbles for the kids, and an air bubble for the adults, so the kids don't keep on yelling in your face. It's a sound-proof bubble. And there's a special door, and it's kind of an egg shell kind of thing. And it has aviatic [aviation-like] brakes. The seats are red ... they're stainproof, in case the kids spill anything on them. And the kids kind of have a little video game in there, so they don't get bored. And there's kind of a ... you know them green 3D glasses that you can put on? (*Gestures how the glasses wrap around the head.*)

And there are little jet packs on the back, so you can go a bit faster. And the jet pack's rocketed by ... you know that stuff they put in an aeroplane? It's rocketed by that. You can put it on slow-mo, and everything. And it's solar powered. But ... you'll still have fuel. The solar power injects the fuel into it. If you just want slow motion, you just leave it on solar power, 'cause it doesn't go that fast. Especially if you're at night time ... you have to turn it on to ... um fuel, because solar power doesn't work at night. It has to be in the sun. But you can get a battery for the solar power. And ... in case you want to go to San Francisco, and you're in Australia ... there is a little thing here that can take you there. *Draws a red box below the car.* But you have to turn on to your solar power because, say if you went at day, it would be night there. That's the um gravitation booth. It has a little blue monitor on it. And it tells how much gravity. So, after San Francisco, you have to get under the car while it's still hovering. Like, you need to get the battery put in again.

John describes the hover boards that people use to fly around, which makes it handy to get into the three-tiered shopping centre. Of particular interest is his description of a 'geographic model' on top of the shop (far right), a theme he develops further toward the end of the narrative. In my interpretation, it is like a hologram – it is three-dimensional and can move in space and pass through objects.

Say if it's got a little sign here *draws an upright shark on top of the building* that sign can come out. Say this is a shark attack, or attacking sharks, it can move, like a geographic model. (*Gestures out and back in the air.*) And it'll be a geographic model, and it [the sign's message] will have all about how you can kill them [sharks], and why you shouldn't, why sometimes you should kill them. It can move out and forward. Say if a man is standing there [at the bottom of the building], it'll come out and kind of ... (*makes large arm gesture*) it'll kind of come up and eat you, but you won't feel it, because it's just a geographic model.

John also applies scientific knowledge when describing cameras, lasers and force fields in relation to surveillance at the bank and the special technology that the police use to catch criminals.

And the banks [building on the left] have more lasers, to track down the bad people that are coming in. The bank's not that big because they can store the money in other banks. *Adds a surveillance camera to the right-hand side of the bank.* And they have special lasers that come down, like a big wall that you can't go through. It comes down to the very bottom of it. *Adds a square to the left side of the bank, with a surveillance camera suspended from its roof.* And, just in case they come in by the back, up here, there's a little camera, and that laser there will go from the back to the front, and from the front to the back. And if there's two people coming from the back and the front, the lasers will split in half and cover both areas. And the bank also has a good advertisement. You see, the people get fooled. They have a safe in there. *Draws a safe on top of the bank.* And if anyone tries to get in, it'll have that [arch] over it, 'cause they'll fool everyone. Because the safe inside the bank isn't filled with any money, only the cash registers are. But this [safe up here] is filled with money. So, they trick them, by putting their money on the top [of the bank].

But in case they're a bit curious, they'll go in there, and that'll stop 'em. *Adds radiating lines to the arch over the safe.* By the force field around there. It'll stop 'em, say if they're only a metre close. A special ray'll hit them and kind of knock them out, but not seriously … just … put them asleep … 'til the police get there. 'Cause the police have got this special dart. If no one sees the man, he'll sleep forever. But the police have got this special dart that they can put in him and stop him from sleeping.

John displays knowledge of other scientific concepts associated with cloning, and his six-and-a-half year old mind frame gives his description a delightful personal spin:

And there's a special kind of a cat. In case one of your favourite cats died, they can get it cloned in a special cloning place. And you can still have your cat back. You should, once you get your cat, you should clone it. Because then you can have another one of it. And the one that's cloned, it won't die. Because it's … had put in this special stuff. It'll [cloning] even work on … on plants. In case, if you have a really good snapdragon, you can keep that.

A detailed description of the tree-house near the bank, which serves as a safe place where children can play while their parents are at the bank or 'pokis' (Australian slang for gambling places with poker machines), leads to an elaboration of the tunnel below it. This appears to stimulate a further scientific idea.

[The tree] it's hollow in the middle. 'Cause now they've got a special machine that can make it hollow. They put this machine around it and it kind of like sucks all the inside out. You can do that with buildings, if you want to have a big hole through the building, so people can get out if there is a fire. For doctors, they can apply it to people, if they need to get something out that's in there [inside people].

Then John draws a dome over the city, with associated concepts of temperature control and cyclone protection, and special boots that people can wear to fly.

And ... they've got a new technology. Here's the sun and that's all the clouds and everything. And there's a special kind of a roof, over the city [undulating lines]. It's in all different colours 'cause people have spray painted it. Graffiti (*gestures swirling motion across the page, following the line of the roof*). So, in case you're getting a bit cold (*grabs the sides of the desk and shivers*), it'll ... kind of [be like] one of them warmers in a house. Some cities have it, some cities don't. All the major cities have it. Like, in the middle of ah ... Brisbane, kind of major cities. And all the capitals, they have them. Keeps it cool in summer and warm in winter. But say if it's really hot in winter, it'll get cool. 'Cause it can feel the wind [temperature outside] from in here. And they keep on changing when they can feel the different winds. And if ... say if there's a cyclone coming, the cyclone will only like just shake it. So it won't rip anything to bits. And, say if a cyclone comes, and you're out of here [outside the dome] because you're flying somewhere ... and a cyclone comes, it won't hurt you 'cause you'll have these special boots on. And you can fly all the way to the place you're going, and you'll just go through the cyclone without getting hurt ... or twisted round.

Returning to his earlier concept of the 'geographic model' (i.e., holographic shark), John draws a force field that people can pass through without injury. The artist applies principles of *anthropomorphism* when creating a human-like character – it has human qualities and abilities but is 'geographic'.

And, sometimes ... if a kid wants to cross the road, and cars might be in his way, there's a special road that goes over the cars. It's a kind of a force field that they can go through, but he's in the force field, so he won't get hurt. They [cars] can go through him but he won't get hurt.

He's kind of a geographic model. And there's kind of a little suit that he can put on and ... he is geographic. No he doesn't have a suit on at all. He *is* a geographic model. Even if he's real, he'll look like this. He can just speak, but he won't have any face. You won't be able to see his face or anything; he can just speak to you like this. He's got this special speaker. And, say if he's in the bank, and he wants to walk over to the shop, but the truck's too big, he can just run through cars and everything, and go to the shop.

This 'geographic' quality is also applied to cars, enabled through a device that drivers attach to the fronts and backs of their cars, so they can pass through each other in the event of an accident.

> If a car ran into another car ... every time it gets crushed ... your car will turn into a geographic model. Not many people have it, but I'll just do it on this car. You have to buy it. A special thing on its bonnet. So, the car will just hit that thing first. There's a special thing at the back too that will hit them. And if two cars both have these they'll just go through each other. And they can just keep on driving. If that little yellow thing gets crushed, it'll **bmfff** come up again, kind of like a balloon. And your car will be a geographic model all the time. And you won't know it 'til you crash.

John's visual narrative, similar to those of Ethan's and Jacob's, was played out on a seemingly impersonal plane of pictorial fantasy. Their characters had no individual personality. Instead, they were embodiments of abstractions, presented in a *prototypical* fashion. The characters were narrated in third person, as in a commentary, where opinions and descriptions were presented from an *omniscient* point of view.

Yet, in some ways, John, Ethan and Jacob could impersonally 'be' *everyone* and *no-one* at once. The artists' voicing of people, objects and events allowed them to assume some element of their fictional selves. Characters were *spoken about* using words like 'he', 'that person', 'some-one' or 'they', and events and objects were *spoken through* the artist, described indexically as 'this' or 'there'. In John's narrative above, when describing the anthropomorphic figure, he changes his mind about the person having to wear a suit to be 'geographic', saying that 'He is a geo-graphic model. Even if he's real, he'll look like this'. John readily applied fantasy to create fictional characters that bore some resemblance to personal experience, but his sci-fi knowledge liberated him to morph reality, to create fictional characters in a fictional world.

Inspired by models of popular media and personal events, the content of older boys' artworks, in particular, often included spacecrafts, missiles, force fields, sporting events, robots, aliens and characters influenced by favourite DVD, TV and digital-game characters. Proportionately, more boys than girls tended to use action-packed sci-fi forms to enact skirmishes between characters and machines, often through the use of sophisticated technology. This often involved movement upon the page – interactions between objects and charac-ters that enlivened, located and relocated the action at will, to suit the author's unfolding narrative. Whether this was a result of the topic, 'Futures', which may have inspired such themes and forms of representation, or whether other factors played a role in boys' and girls' visual narratives will be explored next.

Form and gender

Golomb (2004) noted that, when children draw self-selected topics, plots of power, destruction and victory appeal mostly to boys who 'reveal an intense concern with warfare, acts of violence and destruction, machinery and sports contests' (p. 160). Certainly, there were many examples of such themes arising in the boys' artworks in this book, which were associated with:

- *Violence* (e.g., shooting a man, Chapter 4), *greed* (e.g., Mr Grouch, Chapter 4), *crime* (e.g., robbing a house, Chapter 4; jailing a criminal, Chapter 5; chasing a drug-smuggling alien, Chapter 6) and *crime surveillance* (e.g., Semi-Taxi and Sky Patrol, Chapter 5).
- *Machinery* (e.g., lifting off from Earth, Chapter 1; Time Machine and Driver Training, Chapter 2; tape-recorder, Chapter 3; road works and backhoeing, Chapters 3 and 5; remote control car, Chapter 4; space capsule breaking away, Chapter 4; lawn mower, Chapter 5; and cranes, Chapter 5), and
- *Sporting events* (e.g., Olympic medallists, Chapter 4; Olympic games and terrorism, Chapter 5).

The heroes in these boys' works were policemen, vehicle drivers and athletes. But not all of the themes of boys' artworks were violent, or focused on machines and sports. Other themes included:

- *Life–death* – kids are 'more' (Chapter 2),
- *Animals* – cat, dog, Mop and Mill; family with dog (Chapter 3),
- *Generosity* – giving Mum a diamond (Chapter 4),
- *Fame* – a rock star (Chapter 4),
- *Fantasy* – magic birds and animals to help Santa and Jesus (Chapter 6),
- *Conservation* – saving the dying park (Chapter 6),
- *Safety* – 'geographic' cars passing through each other and flying boots to get you out of a cyclone (Chapter 6).

By comparison, the compositions of girls generally tended to be less action-packed and more serene. Girls generally depicted tranquil scenes, such as family life, social relations, friendships, nature, children at play and romance. As was found in Golomb's (2004, pp. 162–163) studies of children's self-selected drawings, girls' themes often were derived from fairytales, and animals assumed centre stage. Some examples from the artworks in this book were:

Figure 6.6   Singing in the Stadium (girl, 8.3)

- *Family life* and related matters such as *giving birth* (e.g., in hospital, Chapter 2), *marriage* (e.g., in church, Chapter 3), *family and friends* (e.g., sisters, cat and Mum, Chapter 3), *conservation in the home* (e.g., multiple scenes in one work, Chapter 3) and a *family living on a spaceship* (e.g., meeting fierce aliens, Chapter 6),
- *Playing* (e.g., with computer games, Chapter 4; with a dog, Chapter 5),
- *Animals* (e.g., koala being run over by a car, Chapter 4; blind man with guide dog, Chapter 5),
- *Nature* (e.g., leaving Earth because of the depletion of forests, Chapter 3), and
- *Fantasy* (e.g., fairy in garden, Chapter 2; clicking together love hearts to get away from a flood, Chapter 4; king and queen aliens with a baby boy, Chapter 6).

The heroes in girls' works were an Olympic equestrian athlete (Chapter 1), a police officer handcuffing a criminal (Chapter 2) and singers in the stadium (Chapter 6, see Figure 6.6). Golomb (2004) found that, in girls' self-selected topics, ambition was expressed through themes that touched on stardom, fashion, beauty, fame and popularity. The example in Figure 6.6 (girl, 8.3) centres on stardom, with the artist depicted as singing on stage, with two other friends in the wings (above/backround), watching her perform. The artwork also includes empathy for a disabled friend, who is also one of the stars.

And there is another friend I haven't drawn yet. A best friend, and she is going to play the guitar. Lucy. She suffers from spina bifia. I'll draw a wheelchair. And I'll draw spots for people [the audience]. The seats aren't filled up yet. I won't do all the seats … I like songs like 'I Can't Fight the Faith'. Sometimes I shut my door and pretend I am a singer [on stage], and it makes me feel like a hero.

The ideological content of many girls' works included crime prevention, safety, life–death, marriage, procreation and the conservation of natural resources. But girls' artworks also included:

- *Vehicles* (e.g., busy city with traffic lights, Chapter 4),
- *Sport* (e.g., swimming; trampolining; riding horses, Chapter 5), and
- *Space travel* (e.g., visiting other planets, Chapter 6) with embodied content of 'moving away' from the planet, leaving behind flames and pink swirling wind from the spaceship's motion.

Animals were prominent in other girls' artworks that were not shown in this book, such as a dancing cat wearing clothes, and a girl's bedroom filled with animals that she described as a zoo in her bedroom. The following girl's (8.3) narrative about animals and her being the owner of a Nature Reserve was particularly metaphysical and spiritual.

The animals like it [here] because you never die, and not many people come here. I knew that there would be like a … like a fire would happen. Because … like I think they [the animals] are talking to me, so that's why I know. The animals here never have fights. And there are poisonous snakes, but they don't bite.

Although both genders depicted allegoric ideas, such as heroes and themes of bravery, security, safety and justice, the form in which these were developed and expressed varied. The writing of Rabiger (2008) has provided me with insights on how features in children's visual narratives are similar to two different forms of film – cinematic and theatrical. Neither of these forms is better or more legitimate than the other; they just use content and narrative in different ways. I will describe each briefly, drawing on Rabiger's descriptions of film to illustrate analogies to young children's visual narratives.

Form: analogies to cinematic and theatrical film

The *cinematic film*, which is analogous to John's visual narrative in this chapter, and Ethan's and Jacob's from Chapter 5, 'builds its dramatic units by using short action scenes' (Rabiger, 2008, p. 273) to advance the story, narrated more by action and images than by dialogue. Like the director of a film, the child artist 'works at designing action, behavior, composition, and editing juxtapositions' (p. 273). Similar to the genres of thriller, science fiction, action and adventure, such visual narratives embody themes and approaches that can be alternatives to realism. Like audiences of such films, the authors of action-packed visual narratives 'lose themselves' by identifying with the hero and the energizing sense of excitement at each step. The forward momentum and anticipation leads to wondering, 'what's next?' Yet, as described earlier, the child's chronology of events is driven by the spontaneous unfolding of the plot, and its content may be reordered and revisited. This is largely because, as in cinema, the child's visual narrative hinges on the setting and situations in his/her telling of events. Rabiger elaborates that in such *plot-driven* cinema, 'the sheer movement of events usually compensates for any lack of depth or complexity in the characters' (p. 130).

By contrast, the plot of *theatrical film* tends to be 'lighter or even invisible' (Rabiger, 2008, p. 186); the momentum 'comes from the needs and imperatives of the main characters' (p. 130). Such *character-driven* genres include buddy films or TV family shows or docudramas. These genres explore the experiences of friendships and family matters and tell their story 'mainly through dialogue scenes' (Rabiger, 2008, p. 273). The artwork presented earlier in this chapter about the family travelling to different planets and encountering fierce aliens along the way, is an example of this. The plot is light, and in some ways, the artwork is like an episode of a TV family show, where the characters work through concerns such as avoiding the fierce aliens (i.e., leaving the planet if the aliens happened to be there during the family's holiday).

However, as discussed earlier, the narratives of children's artworks do not contain the type of dialogue that one finds in normal conversation or in film or theatre. Rather, the child implies dialogue associatively, by depicting characters doing things that are organic to the worlds they inhabit. These depictions generally are talked about descriptively, rather than as conversations between characters, as in the example below (Figure 6.7). This girl's (6.1) plot, which also contains fantasy, centres around the sole depicted figure, the mother, who discusses her daughters but they are not drawn. The artist sets the scene through contextual images and develops the characters by describing their physical and sensual qualities. This leads into magic-based abstractions of the binary concepts of aggression–protection and fighting–forgiving.

Figure 6.7   The Magic Story (girl, 6.1)

This is me and I am spreading out a picnic blanket for the children. She [I] has trendy shoes like we wear now, but they don't wear out. Her dress sometimes gets wet, and if she tries to rip it, it is too hard to rip. And when you spin around it makes a pretty noise.

Fish in the pond [right hand side] are invisible. When you go in there, there is crocodiles, and they are invisible too.

My girls are over at the swings. Katie and Sophie. One's 5 and one's 10. Their hair is really um good. When you brush it, it goes like silky. And Sophie, her hair she can think, and then she can ... [magically] change her hair to go blue or green or red. She just likes different coloured hair.

When someone has been naughty and she wants to strangle someone, she has got a magic hand and has got rings and just <u>punches</u> them in the head. When a baddie comes she just tells her sister and her sister tells me, and then I have got blue eyes and stuff comes out [of my eyes], and it follows them and they go away. She doesn't do this to her friends though, because she doesn't want anything to happen to them. She got these magic powers when she was a little baby in her Mummy's tummy. And she was powerful in her brain and neck and all that.

Sometimes the girls fight, and they get a magic flower [left-hand side of the page] and they just stop the fight and are friends again. The magic flowers never grow, they are just as they are, they never die off. And if she wants to clean up she just goes like this (*closes her eyes*) and the washes-up go into a drawer. Just closes her eyes. Then everything washes up.

This girl's *character-driven* plot centres on the imperatives of the mother and her children and explores the experiences of friendships and family matters. But it also includes other, often abstract themes centred on the following:

Figure 6.8   Living, Dying, Evolution and War (girl, 8.5)

- *Senses* – her dress may get wet; when she spins around, the dress makes a pretty sound,
- *Aesthetics* – trendy shoes and silky hair of different colours,
- *Longevity* – shoes that don't wear out, a dress that can't be ripped, magic flowers that never grow or die,
- *Good versus bad* – the mother protects her children and uses her magic powers on bad people but not on friends,
- *Fantasy* – fish and crocodiles are invisible, and
- *Magic* – the daughter can change her hair colour by 'thinking it', the mother has magic rings that can punch people and eyes that can telepathically ward off danger (powers that she developed in the brain/neck before birth), the magic flowers stop children from fighting, and the mother can wash the dishes and put them in the drawer just by closing her eyes and 'thinking it'.

Sensory-based issues that centre on the concept of longevity are also explored in the final example of a character-based plot (Figure 6.8). This drawing-telling does not involve fantasy, but instead explores a theme that would not commonly be raised in typical school art experiences – life and death. The visual narrative contains many concepts associated with life (e.g., baby animals), possible death of animals (e.g., having her dog 'put down') and her objection to the prospect of her dog being castrated (so it can't have babies). Ultimately, this leads to abstract concepts of conservation and evolution. The artist (girl, 8.5) includes paraphrasing of conversations she has had with her parents, which in some ways are like dialogues, but the characters and setting of the content discussed are not drawn – the information is related as a 'side story'. Indeed, much of the narrative is like a philosophical reflection that goes deeply into the past and projects into the future, with the core theme centring on living creatures.

Early in the work the artist comments:

> 'I'd love to have a tree house like that. I keep on thinking that my Granddad would build one, before he went to hospital. Because he got this sort of cancer thing, 'cept it's not a sun cancer, it's a different kind of cancer'.

This personal concern for her Granddad's health may have subconsciously influenced her to reflect on deeper issues, which she explores initially through a discussion about her pets, but later expands to more abstract concepts.

> I'll have one cat and guinea pigs. I don't know why my pets all died but. Except one died because I didn't feed it for a while. And the others, we don't know what happened to them. I'm not going to be a vet, because sometimes they have to give dogs needles [to put them to sleep]. My dad hates mice ... and cats. That's why we only had one because he found the cat in the middle of the road. And so he brang him home and put the welder beside its ears, and that's how we found out it was deaf ... so we kept it. So it couldn't hear the cars coming past and all that. Otherwise he could have got run over. He must have been out there in the middle of the road for a long time then. But the parrot that Mum said, um she saw squashed down in the ground, she said, 'I wish I hadn't said oops'. 'Cause she said that because she saw it. But she said she didn't run over it.
>
> My favourite animals are dogs. Some aren't intelligent Mum says. My dog, Patchy, doesn't ask; he just takes everything. 'Cause he comes in the house and takes things off the table and takes it out. He's fully grown now, but he still does it. And Mum said if he gets sick one more time we are going to put him down. That's what she said last time, because he broke his leg or something, ah, I forget what. And then he got this sort of ... he got sick, and the vet said that most dogs have died from it. So he's lucky to be alive.
>
> And I asked Mum, 'Can we not get Patchy to not have babies [not castrate him]. Can we get him to have babies?' He's a boy and um I want him to be a father. And Mum said, 'Well we should just make him run away because we won't have the pups anyway'. And I said, 'I don't care'.

'Cause there's this dog that always comes round to our place, and I don't know if it's a girl or a boy.

And, you know, there might be different animals in the future, 'cause there were in the past. Like, er … an elephant, except that it doesn't have skin, it has fur. That'd be a good one (*laughs*). I wonder in the future if some animals that live on the ground now are going to live in the air or something. My dad says dogs don't live as long as people. But [in the future] like people might be able to grow older than they can now. Then we'd get to see lots of things. But we might even have to sleep outside. Because … you know like the dinosaurs? 'Cause you know how um … like … in some parts of the world they're dying and that? 'Cause it, like war, um, might come to Australia.

This artist's identification with animals was depicted through her empathy with the deaf cat, her annoyance with her dog's bad manners and the associated concern that he might be put down before he can become a father. She applies concepts of life and death by referring to the extinction of dinosaurs and mammoths and the prospect of ground-based animals evolving into air-borne species. By analogy, the girl expands on her awareness of dog versus human life years and explores the prospect of future medical science extending human life-spans. Although she does not use abstract terminology directly, and the thread that links the concepts of life–death, extinction–evolution and longevity is not articulated, the girl shows evidence of deep abstract thought, which concludes with concepts associated with poverty, war and globalization.

This girl's narrative and those of many girls' throughout this book often were more character-based than event- or plot-based, compared to boy's works (which were more event- or plot-based). However, there are exceptions to this trend, which seem to be aligned with the artist's authorial intentions and the way he/she wants the work to function. Indeed, gender differences seem to be a stylistic concern.

Stylization

In film, stylized environments such as in Fritz Lang's *Metropolis* (1926), become a leading component of the discourse. Similarly, a striking visual approach can be created in children's visual narratives through decor, light and location. Such visual elements reinforce intended meanings and affect how we expect characters to behave (Rabiger, 2008, p. 193). Stylization can also function metaphorically and connote concepts such as vastness, through the use of large,

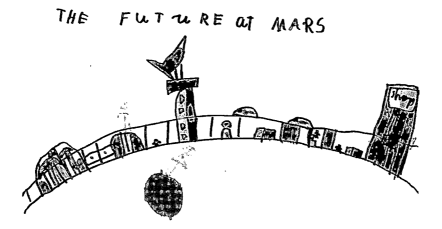

Figure 6.9   The Future at Mars (boy, 7.8)

empty spaces, or tranquillity through light and colour in clouds, as in the following two examples.

In Figure 6.9 this boy's (7.8) stylized environment is set on Mars, where: cars run on a monorail, the top of a highrise building is a rocket launcher 'to pick up more people to bring back to Mars', and a TV station and large disc/aerial (below the high rise) sends waves 'all the way to Earth, and they get their TV on stations here'. People live underground and have to wear space suits unless they are in the rocket.

The artwork is essentially scenery-based, with very few events or characters. It functions in a similar way to a documentary about people living on Mars, with descriptive content explaining what this would be like. The artist applies what he knows about the Earth's nature, and features concepts of oxygen and gravity and the importance of greeneries to survive on Mars.

> This is a greenery house ... and ... they get oxygen from the trees. And nearly every house has a greenery. They took them [the trees] from Earth and brought them up ... to space ... Gardeners can go along the tunnel into their house to plant some more plants. There is grass and everything, 'cause it's like you're back here [on Earth], only it's under cover.

Similarly, an emphasis on nature is a strong element of the girl's (8.5) artwork in Figure 6.10. Like the previous artwork, the scenery is a prominent feature. But compared to *The Future at Mars*, which is technology-based and object focused, in this work the characters drive the plot. The artist drew herself at the age of 59, beside her

Figure 6.10   The Sunrise of Life (girl, 8.5)

lifelong best friend. These two figures are in a central position, standing with walking canes beneath a highly colourful sunrise. Although the narrative centres on growing old, the prominent sunrise, coupled with a back-to-nature ideology, creates an atmospheric, 'spiritual' context that features animals, fish, plants and flowers. The peacefulness of the setting and its positive associations with old age make it tempting to metaphorically call the artwork *The Sunrise of Life.*

> I'm drawing the grass in the garden and a rose bush [far right]. It's got some roses on it. And I'm picking flowers and I've got some nice ferns. I'm going to draw myself when I get big. I'm old. It's a walking stick. I'm about 59. And this is Brooke. She's old like me. We've been friends forever. She's got brown hair. Long curly hair ... blowing out everywhere. Out to enjoy the world. Brooke has got a blue tracksuit. Now I'll draw a dog with a bone, because it likes its bone. The dog is gold. It's a golden dog, so I'll draw it yellow. And I'm going to draw a fishpond, because we like to keep fish. We've got some purple fish, some red fish and a multi-coloured fish. And the cover [on the fish pond] is made out of clear glass so we can see through it, to see all the fishes. And the red fish is putting its head up to say hello. We're in the country, and we've got some horses in the paddock. And my horse is called Star and Brooke's is King.

> Winter's almost over but there's some blue sky, and it's early in the morning. And it's colder in the mornings I guess, so that's why I need my

tracksuit. There is some maroon sky. I think I have to draw some red in the clouds so that it is the sun making them bright. The sun is making the colourful sky.

We didn't like the city because it was too noisy, so we moved from the city to the country. And we just wanted to go back there. 'Cause that was the way our life was meant to be. We only get up early once a week, otherwise we don't get enough sleep. I'll call this 'Peaceful Morning' because there's quiet in the country and it's so beautiful in the peace and quiet.

Similar to the visual narrative of the mother with magic powers, this drawing-telling includes sensory-based, aesthetic issues (e.g., picking flowers and ferns, wearing tracksuits because the morning is cold, leaving the city because it was too noisy, finding beauty and peace in the quietness of the country). It also includes fantasy, such as the women 'communicating' with the fish ('the red fish is putting its head up to say hello'). A striking example of metaphor is the artist's description of Brooke's long, curly, blowing hair, which is 'Out to enjoy the world'. Longevity is also expressed by her description that she and Brooke have been friends 'forever'.

The stylized environments within this and the previous drawing are a leading component of the children's discourse. The decor, location and visual elements reinforce the intended meanings metaphorically, such as connoting the vastness and technical sophistication of life on Mars or the tranquility of living in the country.

Summary

The signs that children use to communicate their imaginary worlds often contain underlying ideologies which are denoted by their drawn characters, settings, objects and events and connoted through deeper meaning. Some of the ideas in children's visual narratives may be adapted from media such as film, theatre or cartoons, which often include tensions between what characters want and what impedes them from acting on something. Popular media often draws upon the themes of traditional forms of myth and allegory, which frequently depict the interplay between binary oppositions, such as good/evil, dominance/submission, real/imaginary or natural/supernatural. Children use similar themes in their drawings, not only to create a gripping plot, but also to make sense of the world and their experiences. By doing so, they develop personalized theories, explore moral imperatives such as right and wrong and push beyond the boundaries of realism. The plots of children's visual narratives provide a frame in which they can enact their senses of life's causes and effects and, through fantasy, transcend their characters' constraints, arising triumphantly.

Children's use of allegoric themes such as bravery, security, safety and justice involves making suggestive resemblances between a visible event or character and another, more abstract level of meaning. Quasi-human figures offer children the opportunity to polarize between real and fantasy worlds, often through metaphorical leaps. But because the characters, objects and events may be prototypical rather than specific, the child's narrative may be presented from an omniscient point of view, spoken in the third person in an impersonal manner. The child can 'be' everyone or 'no one' at once.

However, the content and form of such plots is influenced by whether the visual narrative is plot-driven or character-driven. Both boys and girls used each of these types of forms. Plot-driven drawings tended to build dramatic units by using short action scenes, similar to the filmic genres of the thriller, science fiction, action or adventure. By contrast, the plot of character-driven drawings was lighter and generally explored experiences such as friendships and family matters, similar to the genres of buddy films or TV family shows. Attending to the young artist's authorial intentions and what the content and form communicates helps us to accept both forms as valid and important meaning-making frameworks for children to experience and share their 'realities' with us.

Reflections

Watch an animated film created for children and deconstruct the binary oppositions that were depicted, such as good/evil, bravery/cowardice, masculine/feminine, nature/history and other concepts. Consider the following:

1. Who were the heroes and antagonists? Were there anthropomorphic figures?
2. What were the plot points and complications that lead to tension, anticipation, suspense or surprise?
3. What references were made to other texts such as storybook characters, or themes, settings, object or events from other genres?
4. How is the film similar to a 'morality play'?
5. Reflect on how popular media influences children's concepts of self, their theory building and their understanding of their worlds.

Additional readings

Barthes, R. (1977). *Image–music–text.* London: Fontana.

Bettelheim, B. (1976). *The uses of enchantment.* Random House, UK: Vintage Books.

Egan, K. (1999). *Children's minds, talking rabbits and clockwork oranges: Essays on education.* New York: Teachers College Press.

Rabiger, M. (2008). *Directing: Film techniques and aesthetics* (4th ed.). Burlington, MA: Focal Press.

7

Implications for Teaching

Figure 7.1   Houses and Drawings (girl, 5.5)

At the completion of this chapter, you should be able to:

1. Describe creativity in relation to fundamental principles presented in this book,
2. Understand how the schooling process often is at odds with young children's imaginative and creative dispositions, and
3. Reflect on what you have learned about children and drawing in relation to a pedagogy that honours the imagination and creativity in children's lives.

'When I grow up I'll draw and get a new house' (girl, 5.5)

As illustrated in the comment by the preschool girl above, in relation to her drawing (see Figure 7.1) she assigns equal importance to the future events, as an adult, of buying a house and continuing to draw. Although art is such an important part of her life as a preschool child, many may be sceptical about whether this disposition will continue into adulthood. Daniel Pink, for instance, in his book *A whole new mind: Why right-brainers will rule the future* (2006) relates the story of how Gordon MacKenzie, a longtime creative force at Hallmark Cards, opened each talk with children by telling them he was an artist and asking 'How many artists are there in the room? ... please raise your hands?' (p. 68).

> The responses always followed the same pattern. In kindergarten and first-grade classes, every kid thrust a hand in the air. In second-grade classes, about three-fourths of the kids raised their hands, though less eagerly. In third grade, only a few children held up their hands. And by sixth grade, not a single hand went up. The kids just looked around to see if anybody in the class would admit to what they'd now learned was deviant behaviour. (Pink, 2006, pp. 68–69)

The irony of this is that the schooling process, as children progress through the system, deprecates the innate abilities of children to use their imaginations and to develop creative thought through art. Yet, from a very early age, children instinctively make marks to symbolically explore concepts and discover meaning. Indeed, by the time they enter preschool, most children are experienced makers of meaning and have developed a repertoire of signs that they employ with great ease and considerable enjoyment. The act of making marks on any available surface, be it the steamy windows of a car, the surfaces of sand or a blank piece of paper, seems to be as natural to young children as breathing, sleeping and laughing. It is a fundamental form of creativity and expression and a key precursor to learning sign making in other forms of communication. Art allows young children to share their inner worlds in ways that can't be as easily communicated through other forms. Why, then, should such a fundamental form of knowledge creation and communication be taken away from young children?

Most children arrive at preschool with a desire to continue to play and to make art. Typically, preschool classrooms offer a range of resources for art making such as painting, drawing, constructing and building, which are accepted as forms for exploratory play and a starting point for emergent writing and graphic speech. But often children are left to their own devices to create, because teachers often see art as *expression* rather than *communication* (Kress, 1997). Alternatively, free drawing is replaced by craft activities, which centre on 'socialization into following directions and routinized processes and products' (Bresler, 2002, p. 182). As Bresler points out, such experiences offer little opportunity for children's imagination, deep experiences or sense of ownership, because children do not participate in self-derived sign making and reflection (p. 178). Although drawing offers a way of representing meaning and a tool for learning, Anning laments that, 'in school children retreat to the safety of a narrow and limited range of drawing behaviours preserving any interest in exploratory types of drawing for out of school settings' (Anning, 1999, p. 171).

When drawing is not taken seriously, adults may simply collect the works of children, taking little interest in the learning that took place or listening to and watching the meaning that is being communicated. Perhaps this disembodiment of the creator from the act of creation is linked to the proliferation of visual media in society today and the relatively unattached role of many participants of the arts, where they are simply members of the audience or consumers of products, rather than producers of creative output. Chandler (2002) elaborates on this point:

> Most people feel unable to draw or paint, and even among those who own video-cameras not everyone knows how to make effective use of them. This is a legacy of an education system which still focuses almost exclusively on the acquisition of one kind of symbolic literacy (that of verbal language) at the expense of most other semiotic modes (in particular the iconic mode). (p. 219)

But, as discussed throughout this book, what we generally call the imagination and creativity are mental capacities that are evoked, stimulated and developed through artistry. *Children's drawings involve the depiction of content through graphic and body-based action, while talking about aspects of their artworks and the processes of their creation through a free-form type of narrative.* The depiction of imaginary worlds while dialoguing with the materials is akin to play. Children discover the power of signs and develop fluid thought processes and skills that equip them to be active creators. We have been in danger of deprecating these important capacities in children and would be wise to preserve them as fully as possible. In a world which is becoming increasingly mechanized, such abilities are what will sustain cultures and develop individuals who can cope with the quickly evolving demands of globalization. Indeed, as Pink (2006) argues, a culture whose inhabitants are afraid to imagine are unlikely to be much good at doing anything well, particularly those things that define and advance culture, such as the creation of literature, the making of art or finding creative breakthroughs in fields such as science or mathematics. He elaborates:

> Today, the defining skills of the previous era – the 'left brain' capabilities that powered the Information Age – are necessary but no longer sufficient. And the capabilities we once disdained or thought frivolous – the 'right brain' qualities of inventiveness, empathy, joyfulness, and meaning – increasingly will determine who flourishes and who flounders. (p. 3)

Pink (2006) replaces the traditional 'left- and right-brain' terminology with 'L-directed' and 'R-directed' thinking. He describes L-directed thinking as involving 'sequential, literal, functional, textual, and analytic' skills which are 'exemplified by computer programmers, prized by hardheaded organizations, and emphasized in schools'; R-directed thinking involves 'simultaneous, metaphoric, aesthetic, contextual, and synthetic' skills which are 'exemplified by creators and caregivers, short changed by organizations, and neglected in schools' (p. 26). Pink makes analogies to cognitive (concept) and social-emotional (touch) abilities, and high levels of each are described as follows.

> High concept involves the ability to create artistic and emotional beauty, to detect patterns and opportunities, to craft a satisfying narrative, and to combine seemingly unrelated ideas into a novel invention. High touch involves the ability to empathize, to understand the subtleties of human interaction, to find joy in one's self and to elicit it in others, and to stretch beyond the quotidian, in pursuit of purpose and meaning. (pp. 51–52)

Ideally, education should nurture 'high concept/high touch' abilities because, as Lev Vygotsky (1978) argues, the mind, unlike the body, takes on in significant degree the shape of what it 'eats' (Egan, 1999, p. 63). What we learn is due to the cognitive and affective tools mediated in education systems and in the culture in which we live. If teachers perceive drawing as being useful only for occupational or recreational purposes, children become cultured only into 'academic' achievement and, consequently, lose out on the challenges offered through art and visual thinking. Ironically, whilst pushing children to perform 'academically' in the early stages of schooling, we underestimate them 'intellectually'. Learning to form and employ visual signs and texts is analogous to the process of learning words and language. Yet if the mediation of art learning simply involves routinized processes, the 'worthwhile meat of art' is substituted with 'cotton candy content', which deprives children of developing the 'ability to form configurational signs' and visual representations (Wilson & Wilson, 1977, p. 11).

A *semiotic* emphasis on sign production will provide a well-rounded 'diet' for young children's learning. Through the act of creating visual narratives, children: (a) generate mental images and depict these through configurational signs: (b) shape imaginative narratives; and (c) use gesture and expressive vocalisms to enhance and extend their meaning. Such skills peak in the early years but typically go into decline later in childhood, and most evidently in adulthood. If the use of these sign systems is not valued, and if there is no provision for their development, they begin to atrophy.

If our educational aim is to produce 'high concept/high touch' individuals, we must attend to cultivating the ground from which that grows. This requires a re-appraisal of what is valued in the schooling system, and whether the educational approaches reach all children. As Anning notes, in schools, 'children who in Howard Gardner's terms favour visual or kinaesthetic modes of learning (Gardner, 1993a, b) begin to be marginalized' (Anning, 1999, p. 169). Individuals with artistic capacities, even at a high level of competence, often are considered 'second stream', 'non-academic', 'dumb'. This disempowers children from engaging in representational practices that are critical to imagination, meaning-making and creativity and overlooks how these experiences strengthen children's abilities in other sign systems, such as reading, mathematics and science.

Acculturation through education should offer an array of symbolic forms of representation for children to use. Yet education is biased towards *teaching* children the more rule-bound, structured symbol systems, where written letters, words and numbers are seen as a 'higher status' mode of representation than *free composing* through drawing. This fails to recognize that the *multimodal* approach to learning through art 'lets in more meaning'. Through art, children actively *construct* their current and expanding understanding of themselves and their worlds, rather than simply becoming the passive recipients of knowledge. The act of drawing becomes an instrument through which children's processes are played out – they can visualize as well as articulate, depict as well as describe. Art encourages *synaesthesia* by fostering the child's capacity to translate ideas from one mode into another, where imagination and cognition become entwined (Kress, 1997). Kress elaborates that 'the freeing of one will have positive effects on the other ... imagination is dependent on actively moving across media and modes, always going beyond the boundaries set by conventions in a particular mode' (p. 109).

When teachers show an interest in children's drawing strategies, they encourage them to learn what they are ready to learn, not just what curriculum designers deem appropriate for the larger society to learn. Finding time to listen to children's visual narratives may be challenging in teachers' busy schedules, but it is time well spent. Visual narratives offer an opportunity to sit with children and to notice the worlds they create and to savour and preserve the wonders they are discovering. By doing so, teachers develop professional knowledge about how children's thinking and knowing develops and can 'ponder on their work and their interactions with children' (Nutbrown, 2006, p. 23). A serious interest in children's 'semiotic dispositions' and sign-making processes can lead to pedagogies and curricula that are matched with the potentials and abilities of the child (Kress, 1997, p. 13).

As educators, it is a common tenant that we should start where the child is. But, ironically, we often forget that children have imaginations, and that there is a constant dialectical play between what they know and what they imagine. As children already know imagination, play and drawing, this seems to be a very natural entry point for teachers to learn more about the child. Composing through art is the visual equivalent of dramatic play. What is required is our awareness that the child's depictions of people, places, objects and events are 'told' through *graphic action* – mark-making that depicts ideas and feelings on paper in real time. It is a spontaneous unfolding of content that moves in and out of loosely structured themes; a type of thinking which is associated with the openness of *configurational* signs. The child's accompanying running narrative also is free-flowing and open to alteration. Delightfully, it is accompanied with vocalisms, facial expressions and body-based communication, where these and graphic action do the 'talking' of the characters and their experiences.

This is an authentic kind of participation, and a concrete form through which we can observe the workings of the child's imagination and the role of imagery in his/her thinking. Talk, drawing and movement are parallel and mutually *transformative* processes – they enrich and inform each other. Children selectively and frequently move from one mode to another to represent and re-present what they know most effectively. They may choose to draw it, or to tell it or to show it through their bodies – or to combine these modes. Hence, drawing is a constructive process of thinking in action. 'Children draw pictures and tell a story at the same time; they act a role and create their lines as they go along' (Linqvist, 2001, p. 8).

This is similar to what Abbs (2003) describes as '*embodied imagination*' in which the 'life of the spirit' can be shared and developed non-discursively. While drawing, children enter into a transcendent, interpretive space where they can 'tell themselves about themselves' (Geertz, 1971, p. 26). To be present in that space is to witness the internal worlds that children imagine, investigate and make real through the images of their art. Drawing is a means of direct *metaphoric* communication, by investing the materials with the capacity to physically embody the self. By manipulating art materials directly, children's thinking and reasoning is enhanced, which is why art is such an important medium for early cognitive and affective development. It integrates *sensorimotor* and other forms of reasoning, feeling and learning that emerge through the body. *Somatic knowing* involves exchanges between the psyche (mind), the soma (body) and the 'soul'. This is fundamental to all human thinking and feeling.

Early representational drawings are somatic, involving interplays between production and perception and *thinking with the body*. Importantly, they engage creative processes of problem finding/ solving, flexibility, fluency, elaboration, transformation, objectivity/ selectivity and aesthetic appreciation. Children feel at liberty to improvise structures and they find *composing* through art an appealing process, perhaps because it is *not strictly rule-bound*. While composing, children develop a repertoire of marks and a 'grammar' of communication, and refine these through practice. By making an object of their own contemplation, they create a symbolic world. Indeed, thinking in symbols is one of the most sophisticated modes of thought. *Symbols* give shape to formless ideas.

Children's *multimodal* texts involve the signs of speech, image, sound, movement and gesture. While every instance of representation is new and creative, the process also involves applying specific traditions and practices. Our goal is to understand the *signifying practices* that children use as they draw – what the 'small' signs mean in relation to the 'larger' *holistic text*. Lines, shapes, proportions, colours, shading, perspective and composition combine to create integrated meaning. Consequently, we must not only attend to the child's *content* (i.e., themes, people, places, objects, events) but also to the aesthetic and *symbolic form* in which this is communicated.

When tuning into what the child is *doing*, we predominantly assume the role of audience. But in some ways we also serve as a type of playmate with the child, where our comments and questions may become a catalyst that enriches the child's play. Such *joint involvement episodes* (Schaffer, 1992) are relational and interactive. They require empathy with the *reciprocity* that occurs between the child and the materials and with us. Hence, it is important for us to *suspend disbelief* and enter the child's imaginary world and go with the flow.

Because of children's use of *indexical language* while drawing, the inferences we make about their meaning will be based on a combination of intuition, our understanding of children and our knowledge of the medium of drawing. Children's indexical words are used in association with *location* (e.g., this, that, here, there), *spatial relations* (e.g., near, far), *time* (e.g., before, after, now, then), and *identification* (e.g., I, you, he, she, they). So we must attend to whether the child's depicted people, places, objects and events are voiced through *first-person* narration (as if being inside the experience), or through *third-person* narration (as if being outside the experience). The young artist uses multiple voices and may take on many roles, 'being' all of the characters and 'participating' in all the events, similar to how they shift in-and-out of various roles during play. Characters may be spoken *for* or spoken *about* as the child moves between events, and *prototypic ideas* may be used to represent a broad concept like humankind, compassion or heroism.

Yet children's narratives are different to 'stories' that are told after the event. Post hoc renditions are a pale imitation of the vitality of the child's running commentary and the 'soul' of the composition, which is filled with dramatizations as the child 'plays with signs'. Indeed, art, play and sign making are so interconnected that a young child may describe drawing a house as 'building' it, or use the terms 'draw' and 'write' interchangeably. Drawn figures and written letters are given equal *intratextual* status alongside speech bubbles and whoosh lines. Similar to icons in comic books, these devices help anchor the child's meaning: speech bubbles 'voice' the characters and 'audiate' silent action; whoosh lines 'move' or 'animate' objects and characters.

Children depict *dynamic events* and interactions using principles of similarity, proximity, surroundedness and vectors. At the *surface* level, the content denotes a *literal* message, generally focused on the people, places, objects and events. At the *deep* level, abstract concepts, ideas and values connote a *symbolic* message. So understanding children's meaning is not only about looking at *what* is being communicated, but also *how* this is done through the child's use of *aesthetic form*, like shading, bold lines, strong contrasts, angles or framing. Visual metaphors include elements such as: 'warm', 'soft', 'cold' and 'harsh' colours; 'pleasant' wavy lines and 'agitated' angular ones; and visual 'depth'.

Synaesthetically, these expressive facets work in consort. For instance, when children enact the movement of their drawn characters, such as using their fingers to step up the stairs or to cross a river by walking only on the white bits, they are *internalizing actions* of what their own bodies would feel. Similarly, children use *icons* to *graphically enact* movement such as lines or dots to connect or separate figures or objects – the trajectory of a bullet to shoot a man or a line to sever the engine from the capsule of a spaceship. Such icons economically resemble mental images of objects and characters and their actions. But icons also include *vocalism* – the use of sounds to model something through resemblance – like '*drrr*' to imitate the sound of a guitar. There seems to be a fluid integration of the *enactive* mode (representing thoughts through motor response) with the *iconic* mode (transferring mental images into graphic meaning through lines/dots and vocalism). Similar integration occurs when children use *symbols* to represent 'big picture' ideas like patriotism, triumph and heroism by depicting national flags flown at different levels, employing specific colours and marks on athletes' uniforms (e.g., Canadian maple leaf) and drawing a tiered podium on which gold, silver and bronze medallists stand.

Indeed, children's inherent desire to create structure and meaning is a fundamental aspect of human cognition. Through visual narratives, children become a 'cast of one', where they can 'be' the characters 'living' their events while taking on *multiple roles* – artist, scripter, narrator, performer, director, audience and critic. They develop the themes and plots of their play, layering the action and altering the scenery at will through drawing, talking and dramatizing their ideas on paper. The popular media often influences children's artworks, and they 'borrow' from these texts to frame their ideas. Such *intertextuality* involves seeing life through an alternative prism. Yet each child's drawn version of an 'other-wordly reality' involves re-visioning, and the new text that is created carries the child's own personal imprint or style.

Like a film-maker, the child composes and makes aesthetic decisions by taking into consideration matters such as *light* (day/night), *colour* (bright/dull), *sound* (narrative and vocalisms), *action* (gesture and icons), *time* (now, before, after), *space* (front/behind, close/distant, above/below), *orientation* (vertical/horizontal axes) and *structure* (verbal, visual, gestural). Their drawn characters have signifying features (e.g., poses, expressions and gestures) linked to their roles, personal qualities, behaviours and goals. Objects also carry connotations linked to place (e.g., Mars with a rocket launcher and large radar disc), setting (e.g., picnic blanket and magic flower), scenery (e.g., sunrise) and décor (e.g., skull and cross-bones on gate).

Time and space are underpinning features of these artworks. When the content is like a *photo-shoot*, it gives a rather static impression, largely attributed to the frontal orientation of the figures. However, if figures are drawn in action, they are like *freeze-frames*. Two events may occur at the same time and in the same space or at different times in different spaces. However, children may not explicitly elaborate on such temporal-spatial details – either verbally or graphically – but instead, might use gesture to refer to movement in space or to imply content off the page. Children's content may also function in a similar way to *frames* or *scenes*. Indeed, in complex, action-packed drawings, there may be multiple scenes within one work, unified by themes that sustain the plot and move the action along.

The themes of children's work often connote underlying *ideologies* such as bravery, honesty, courage, security and hope. These may be reflected in the *subtexts* of the child's depicted characters, illustrated through their behaviours and the tensions between their inner and outer worlds, such as security and danger, cleverness and stupidity or good and evil. In some ways, the child's visual narrative carries the tradition of oral storytelling, where moral imperatives are conveyed in a single sitting. It contains elements that are similar to myth or allegory and involves playing out of *binary oppositions* such as dominance–submission, real–imaginary or natural–supernatural.

Some may ponder whether making provisions for the exploration of such thoughts and images are appropriate within the school context. Yet, many children soon learn that their drawings in school 'must reflect teachers' view of "childhood innocence" – nothing violent or unseemly' (Anning, 1999, p. 170). Anning elaborates that children learn to conform and produce,

> safe and sanitized portraits of 'people who help us' or observational draw- ings of pot plants or stuffed animals in glass cases borrowed from muse- ums. In most primary school classroom settings, as the children grapple with the conventions of 'school art', their unofficial drawing about what really interests them goes underground. It is done in the safety of their bedrooms or in after school clubs … [where] the children revel in the blood and thunder of monsters, the vulgarity of comic imagery and the expression of raw anger at the futility of war. (pp. 170–171)

Indeed, binary oppositions, like good versus evil, are young children's first logical operation, which helps them categorize and generate order out of complex human experience. This may lead to fantasy- based, exotic characters using *mediating concepts* (Egan, 1999), such as ghosts (which are both alive and dead), aliens (which are both human and other) and natural creatures that use language, wear clothes and have emotions. Such concepts lend a hand to children's development of *abstract* thought and personalized *theories* about the real world in relation to their imaginary ones.

When working within a *mythical, metaphysical* plane, the plot of the child's work acts as a frame for the depiction of his/her own sense of life's causes and effects, but with imaginative dabs of fanciful ideas thrown in. Children, like adults, have a desire to experience, if only temporarily, the world of others. Through drawing, the child can project into the characters' predicaments, and *multiple perspectives* may arise because the child can 'be' each character, and see each differently, though various lenses. Allegoric works make suggestive resemblances between a visible event or character, and another, more abstract level of meaning. The use of quasi-human figures, for instance, offers the child opportunities to polarize between real and fantasy worlds.

Although children's visual narratives often connote deeper ideologies, they may not always involve fantasy. Instead, children may depict humane values such as generosity or friendship and larger concepts such as conservation of the Earth's natural resources, or concerns about matters such as pollution or overpopulation. Depending upon whether the artwork centres on events and is plot-driven, or alternatively on people and is character-driven, the content and narrative will be different. *Plot-driven* visual narratives often build their dramatic units by using short scenes to advance the theme, which are narrated by action and images. The chronology of events is driven by the spontaneous unfolding of events, which may be reordered and revisited through the telling in relation to settings and situations. The sheer movement of events usually compensates for any lack of depth or complexity of the character. By contrast, *character-driven* visual narratives are told mainly through dialogue or implied dialogue associated with the characters' organic doing of things within the worlds they inhabit. These depictions are talked about descriptively, and the plot tends to be lighter or even invisible, centring instead on the characters' experiences.

Although there seems to be a tendency for boys to prefer action-packed and plot-driven forms, with girls choosing more serene, character-driven content, this trend may not be generalized. The choice of form seems largely dependent upon the child's *authorial intentions* and how the artist wants the artwork to *function*. As the drawing task in this research for this book invited children to depict the future, their *style* of representation may have been more metaphoric and fanciful. Certainly, it gave the children 'permission' to access and express their imaginations.

As emphasized through these children's visual narratives, they *conceived* the world, rather than merely rendering it. The children made the learning their own, which can be done 'only if the life of the student is allowed to enter the learning situation' (Thompson, 2002, p. 190). Thompson notes that, because authentic learning through art is fuelled by inner passion, it provides its own motivation. It creates a venue that pushes children outside of themselves while connecting new learning to old. She adds:

> Self-realization is impossible without an entry point, and the entrance cannot happen without an ability to *have* a voice and *hear* the voice of others. In this way the arts, which provide the structuring form to that voice, become instrumental to becoming human ... To deny a child's voice ... is to deny the child's place ... to disclose themselves as human beings. A student without a voice is unknown and unknowable. (p. 191)

I would like to conclude by referring to Abbs's (2003) three reciprocal principles of educational activity that resonate with the content of this book. Abbs's first principle is that *education is existential in nature*. He describes the teacher as a releaser, 'a midwife, aiming to give birth to existential acts of learning and spiritual engagement in the student' (p. 15). Rather than prescribing 'settled narratives of meaning', the purpose is 'to engender a quest in the search of what is not known, of what may never be known, of what is emotionally alluring' (p. 15). This principle not only resonates with the deliberate selection of the drawing topic Futures, to not only take the young artists beyond common, rehearsed schema, but also to liberate the child to imagine and bring into existence something intangible and other-worldly. This respects the child's semiotic disposition for somatic, multimodal forms of representation which may delve into transcendent, mythical and allegoric forms.

Abbs's second principle is that *education is essentially a collaborative activity*. He refers to the plays of Plato, which were elaborations of Socrates' philosophy that the existential act of enquiry arises through 'animated dialogue, in the disciplined narrative of conversation [between] individuals engaged in the common pursuit of understanding' (p. 16). This principle is aligned with the book's emphasis on teachers as interlocutors, surfacing and hearing the voices of children through a genuine form of enquiry and dialogic mediation. Such an approach is tolerant of children's fantasy themes like blood and thunder, violence and despair and concerns for the survival of the planet. Children's visual narratives illustrate their abstract thought, which sometimes explores the depths of controversial issues. In the mutual pursuit of understanding, the interlocutor must be willing to 'go there' with the child.

Abbs's third principle is that *education is always a cultural activity which has to be continuously deepened and extended*. This calls for a 'progressive initiation of the student into the culture of the discipline' which is achieved by grasping the 'intimate connection between symbol and consciousness' (p. 17). This principle resonates with my emphasis on children's creation of artefacts that shape and are shaped by culture. It foregrounds the importance of teachers in understanding not only children and pedagogy, but also the discipline of art – so that they can appreciate the content and form of young children's symbolic communication. Such understanding helps teachers build on children's current knowledge and interests, which can lead to the shared development of an emergent curriculum and continued opportunities for children to construct knowledge rather than simply to be passive recipients of it.

Abbs's final educational principle is *Futures*, a topic that has been a thread throughout this book.

> Education exists to set up a conversation down the ages and across the cultures, across both time and space, so that students are challenged by other ways of understanding and, at the same time, acquiring ever new materials – metaphors, models, ideas, images, narratives, facts – for shaping and reshaping and testing again that never finished process, their own intellectual and spiritual lives. (p. 17)

This principle resonates with the emphasis on education for the future which should foreground 'high concept/high touch' skills to prepare children not only to cope with a quickly evolving, globalized world, but to develop dispositions and skills that will sustain and advance culture. Such skills are inherent in art and creativity, such as fluency, flexibility, transformation, inventiveness, empathy, joyfulness and meaning. These are fundamental processes that children use while crafting imaginative narratives through visual representation, using images and metaphors. The schooling process has been in danger of deprecating these important capacities in children. We would be wise to preserve them as fully as possible.

Summary

The schooling process often is at odds with young children's imaginative and creative dispositions. It is biased toward teaching children the more rule-bound, structured symbol systems, where written letters, words and numbers are seen as a 'higher status' mode of representation over self-derived sign-making, visual thinking and reflection. Ironically, whilst pushing children to perform 'academically' in the early stages of schooling, we underestimate them intellectually.

Often teachers perceive drawing as serving only occupational, expressive or recreational purposes rather than as providing a significant medium for children to explore and communicate their imaginations and creative mental capacities. This overlooks children's competencies to depict ideas and feelings through graphic and body-based action while talking about aspects of their artworks and the processes of their creation. The depiction of imaginary worlds while dialoguing with the materials through a free-form type of narrative is akin to play – it 'lets in more meaning' (Pahl & Rowsell, 2005, p. 43) than the more conventional methods of teaching and learning.

Drawing, as a tool for learning and representing meaning, lets children discover the power of signs and develop fluid thought

(Continued)

(Continued)

processes and skills that equip them to be active creators. Learning to employ visual texts involves generating mental images through configurational signs, shaping imaginative narratives and using gesture and vocalisms to enhance and communicate meaning. If these sign systems are not valued in the schooling process, and there is no provision for their development, they begin to atrophy as children progress through the schooling system. In a world which is becoming increasingly mechanized, such abilities are what will sustain cultures and develop individuals who can cope with the quickly evolving demands of globalization.

Reflections

1.   While reflecting on the content of this book (which was summarized in this chapter) write:

     (a)   Three things you have learnt,
     (b)   Two things you have been reminded of, and
     (c)   One question you still have in relation to each of the following:

           (i)   Young children,
           (ii)   Their art, and
           (iii) Art education pedagogy.

Additional readings

Abbs, P. (2003). *Against the flow: Education, the arts and postmodern culture.* London: Routledge Falmer.

Anning, A. (2002). Conversations around young children's drawing: The impact of the beliefs of significant others at home and school. *International Journal of Art & Design Education, 21*(3), 197–208.

Eisner, E. (2002). What can education learn from the arts about the practice of education? *The encyclopedia of informal education.* Retrieved 3 June 2003 from www.infed.org/biblio/eisner_arts_and_the_practice_of_education.htm

Kress, G. (1997). *Before writing: Rethinking the paths to literacy.* London: Routledge.

Nutbrown, C. (2006). *Threads of Thinking* (3rd ed.). London: Sage.

Pink, D. (2006). *A whole new mind: Why right-brainers will rule the future.* London: Penguin Books.

References

Abbs, P. (2003). *Against the flow: Education, the arts and postmodern culture*. London: Routledge Falmer.

Anning, A. (1999). Learning to draw and drawing to learn. *International Journal of Art & Design Education, 18*(2), 163–172.

Anning, A. (2002). Conversations around young children's drawing: The impact of the beliefs of significant others at home and school. *International Journal of Art & Design Education, 21*(3), 197–208.

Anning, A., & Ring, K. (2004). *Making sense of children's drawings*. Berkshire: Open University Press.

Arnheim, R. (1969). *Visual thinking*. Berkeley, CA: University of California Press.

Arnheim, R. (1974). *Art and visual perception*. Berkeley: University of California Press.

Athey, C. (2007). *Extending thought in young children: A parent-teacher partnership* (2nd ed.). London: Paul Chapman.

Barber, D. (2008). Somaesthetic awareness and artistic practice: A review essay. Book Reviewed: Shusterman, R. (2008). *Body Consciousness: A Philosophy of Mindfulness and Somaesthetics*. Cambridge and New York: Cambridge University Press. *International Journal of Education and the Arts, 9*(1). Retrieved 8 December 2008 from www.ijea.org/v9r1

Barthes, R. (1957/1973). *Mythologies*. London: Fontana.

Barthes, R. (1977). *Image–Music–Text*. London: Fontana.

Best, J. (2000a). Arts, words, intellect, emotion. Part 1: Toward artistic mindedness. *Arts Education Policy Review, 102*(6), 3–11.

Best, J. (2000b). Arts, words, intellect, emotion. Part 2: Toward artistic mindedness. *Arts Education Policy Review, 102*(10), 2–10.

Bettelheim, B. (1976). *The uses of enchantment*. Random House, UK: Vintage Books.

Bhroin, M.N. (2007). 'A slice of life': The interrelationships among art, play and the 'real' life of the young child. *International Journal of Education and the Arts, 8*(16). Retrieved 10 December, 2008 from www.ijea.org/v8n16/

Bresler, L. (2002). School art as a hybrid genre: Institutional contexts for art curriculum. In L. Bresler & C.M. Thompson (Eds), *The arts in children's lives* (pp. 169–183). The Netherlands: Kluwer Academic Publishers.

Brooker, L. (2001). Interviewing children. In G. MacNaughton, S.A. Rolfe & I. Siraj-Blatchford (Eds), *Doing early childhood research: International perspectives on theory and practice* (pp. 162–177). Buckingham: Open University Press.

Bruner, J. (1986). *Actual minds, possible worlds*. Cambridge, MA: Harvard University Press.

Bruner, J. (1996). *The culture of education*. Cambridge, MA: Harvard University Press.

Buckham, J. (1994). Teachers' understanding of children's drawing In E. Aubrey (Ed.), *The role of subject knowledge in the early years of schooling.* (pp. 133–107). London: Falmer Press.

Callery, D. (2001). *Through the body: A practical guide to physical theatre.* New York: Routledge.

Campbell, J. (1991). *The masks of god: Occidental mythology.* New York: Arkana.

Chandler, D. (2002). *Semiotics: The basics.* London: Routledge.

Cox, S. (2005). Intention and meaning in young children's drawing. *Journal of Art and Design Education, 24*(2), 115–125.

Csikszentmihalyi, M. (1988). Society, culture, and person: A systems view of creativity. In R.J. Sternberg (Ed.), *The nature of creativity* (pp. 325–329). New York: Cambridge University Press.

Danesi, M. (2007). *The quest for meaning: A guide to semiotic theory and practice.* Toronto: University of Toronto Press.

Dewey, J. (1934/1988). *Art as experience.* New York: Perigee Books.

Dyson, A.H. (1982). The emergence of visible language: Interrelationships between drawing and early writing. *Visible Language, 6,* 360–381.

Dyson, A.H. (1986). The imaginary worlds of childhood: A multimedia presentation. *Language Arts, 63,* 779–808.

Dyson, A.H. (1990). Symbol makers, symbol weavers: How children link play, pictures, and print. *Young Children, 45*(2), 50–57.

Dyson, A.H. (1993). From prop to mediator: The changing role of written language in children's symbolic repertoires. In B. Spodek, & O.N. Sarachio (Eds), *Yearbook in early childhood education: Language and literacy in early childhood education, vol. 4* (pp. 21–41). New York: Teachers College Press.

Dyson, A.H. (1997). *Writing superheroes: Contemporary childhood, popular culture, and classroom literacy.* New York: Teachers College Press.

Dyson, A.H. (2003). 'Welcome to the jam'. Popular culture, school literacy, and the making of childhoods. *Harvard Educational Review, 73*(3), 326–361. Retrieved 1 December 2004 from www.edreview.org/harvard03/2003/fa03/f03dyson/htm

Eckersley, R. (1992). *Youth and the challenge to change: Bringing youth, science and society together in the new Millennium.* Carlton South: Australia's Commission for the Future.

Eckersley, R. (1999). Dreams and expectations: Young people's expected and preferred futures and their significance for education. *Futures, 31*(1), 73–90.

Eco, U. (1976). *A theory of semiotics,* Bloomington, IN: Indiana University Press.

Egan, K. (1988). *Primary understanding: Education in early childhood.* New York and London: Routledge.

Egan, K. (1992). *Imagination in teaching and learning.* London: Routledge.

Egan, K. (1999). *Children's minds, talking rabbits and clockwork oranges: Essays on education.* New York: Teachers College Press.

Eisner, E. (2002). What can education learn from the arts about the practice of education? *The encyclopedia of informal education.* Retrieved 3 June 2003 from www.infed.org/biblio/eisner_arts_and_the_practice_of_education.htm

Gadsden, V.L. (2008). The arts and education: Knowledge generation, pedagogy, and the discourse of learning. *Review of Research in Education, 32*, 29–61.

Gallas, K. (1994). *The languages of learning: How children talk, write, dance, draw and sing their understanding of the world.* New York: Teachers College Press.

Gardner, H. (1980). *Artful scribbles: The significance of children's drawings.* London: Jill Norman.

Gardner, H. (1983). *Frames of mind: The theory of multiple intelligence.* New York: Basic Books.

Gardner, H. (1993a) *Creating minds: An anatomy of creativity seen through the lives of Freud, Einstein, Picasso, Stravinsky, Eliot, Graham, and Gandhi.* New York: Basic Books.

Gardner, H. (1993b) *Multiple intelligences: The theory in practice.* New York: Basic Books.

Geertz, C. (1971). *Myth, symbol, and culture.* New York: Norton.

Gelb, I.J. (1963). *A Study of Writing.* Chicago: University of Chicago Press.

Golomb, C. (1988). Symbolic inventions and transformations in child art. In K. Egan, & D. Nadaner (Eds), *Imagination and education* (pp. 222–236). Milton Keynes: Open University Press.

Golomb, C. (2004). *The child's creation of a pictorial world* (2nd ed.). London: Lawrence Erlbaum.

Goodman, N. (1976). *Languages of art.* Oxford: Oxford University Press.

Goodman, N. (1984). *Of mind and other matters.* Cambridge, MA: Harvard University Press.

Goody, J. (1977). *The domestication of the savage mind.* New York: Cambridge University Press.

Gross, L.P. (1973). Art as the communication of competence. Paper presented at the Symposium on Communication and the Individual in Contemporary Society. Retrieved 20 March 2007 from www.ucalgary.ca/~rseiler/grosslp.htm

Hodge, R., & Tripp, D. (1986). *Children and television: A semiotic approach.* Cambridge: Polity Press.

Hollyman, D. Jerome Bruner: A web overview. Retrieved 27 July 2008 from http://au.geocities.com/vanunoo/Humannature/bruner.html

Hughes, R. (1996). The case for the elitist do-gooders. *The New Yorker, 72*(32) May.

Hull, G.A., & Nelson, M.E. (2005). Locating the semiotic power of multimodality. *Written Communication, 22*(2), 224–261.

Humphrey, N. (2006). *Seeing red: A study in consciousness.* Cambridge, MA: Harvard University Press.

Jakobson, R., & Halle, M. (1956). *Fundamentals of Language.* The Hague: Mouton.

James, A. & Prout, A. (Eds) (1997). *Constructing and reconstructing childhood: Contemporary issues in the sociological study of childhood* (2nd ed.). London: Falmer Press.

Jewitt, C., & Oyama, R. (2001). Visual meaning: A social semiotic approach. In T. van Leeuwen & C. Jewitt (Eds), *Handbook of Visual Analysis* (pp. 134–156). London: Sage Publications.

Kellman, J. (1995). Harvey shows the way: Narrative. *Art Education, 48*(2), 18–22.

Kendrick, M., & McKay, R. (2004). Drawings as an alternative way of understanding young children's constructions of literacy. *Journal of Early Childhood Literacy, 4*(1), 109–127.

Kline, S. (1993). *Out of the garden: Toys, TV, and children's culture in the age of marketing*. London: Verso.

Kolbe, U. (2000). Seeing beyond marks and forms: Appreciating children's visual thinking. In W. Schiller (Ed.), *Thinking through the arts* (pp. 48–60). Amsterdam: Harwood Academic Publisher.

Kress, G. (1997). *Before writing: Rethinking the paths to literacy*. London: Routledge.

Kress, G. (2000a). Design and transformation: New theories of meaning. In B. Cope, & M. Kalantzis (Eds), *Multiliteracies: Literacy learning and the design of social futures* (pp. 153–161). South Yarra, Victoria: Macmillan.

Kress, G. (2000b). Multimodality. In B. Cope, & M. Kalantzis (Eds), *Multiliteracies: Literacy learning and the design of social futures* (pp. 183–202). South Yarra, Victoria: Macmillan.

Kress, G., & van Leeuwen, T. (1996). *Reading images: The grammar of visual design*. London: Routledge.

Kress, G., & van Leeuwen, T. (1998). Front pages: (The critical) analysis of newspaper layout. In A. Bell & P. Garrett (Eds), *Approaches to media discourse* (pp. 186–219). Oxford: Blackwell.

Labitsi, V. (2007). 'Climbing to reach the sunset': An inquiry into the representation of narrative structures in Greek children's drawings. *International Journal of Education through Art, 3*(3), 185–193.

Lakoff, G., & Johnson, M. (1980). *Metaphors we live by*. Chicago: University of Chicago Press.

Lakoff, G., & Johnson, M. (1999). *Philosophy in the flesh: Embodied mind and its challenge to western thought*. New York: Basic Books.

Langer, S. (1924/1971). *Philosophy in a new key: A study of the symbolism in reason, rite, and art*. Cambridge, MA: Harvard University Press.

Leach, E. (1982). *Social anthropology* (Fontana Master guides). London: Fontana.

Lecoq, J. (2000). *The moving body (le Corps poetique)* (trans. by D. Bradby). London: Methuen.

Lévi-Strauss, C. (1966). *The savage mind*. Chicago: University of Chicago Press.

Lévi-Strauss, C. (1969). *The raw and the cooked*. New York: Harper and Row.

Lewis, C.S. (1982). *Of this and other worlds*. London: Collins.

Linqvist, G. (2001). When small children play: How adults dramatise and children create meaning. *Early Years, 21*(1), 7–14.

Lyons, J. (1977). *Semiotics*, vol. 1. Cambridge: Cambridge University Press.

Matthews, J. (1999). *Helping children to draw and paint in early childhood*. London: Hodder and Stoughton.

Matthews, J. (2001). Children drawing attention: Studies from Singapore. *Visual Arts Research, 27*(1), 13–45.

Matthews, J. (2004). The art of infancy. In A. Kindler, E. Eisner, & M. Day (Eds), *Learning in the visual arts: Handbook of research and policy in art education* (pp. 253–298). Canada: University of British Columbia.

Metz, C. (1974). *Film language: A semiotics of the cinema* (trans. Michael Taylor). New York: Oxford University Press.

Metz, C. (1981). Methodological propositions for the analysis of film. In M. Eaton (Ed.), *Cinema and semiotics (Screen Reader 2)* (pp. 86–98). London: Society for Education in Film and Television.

Nichols, B. (1981). *Ideology and the image: Social representation in the cinema and other media.* Bloomington, IN: Indiana University Press.

Nutbrown, C. (2006). *Threads of thinking* (3rd ed.). London: Sage.

Pahl, K., & Rowsell, J. (2005). *Literacy and education: Understanding the new literacy studies in the classroom.* London: Paul Chapman.

Paley, V. (1981). *Wally's stories.* Cambridge, MA: Harvard University Press.

Paley, V. (1984). *Boys and girls: Superheroes in the doll corner.* Chicago: University of Chicago Press.

Paley, V. (1990). *The boy who would be a helicopter.* Cambridge, MA: Harvard University Press.

Palmer, P. (1986). *The lively audience: A study of children around the TV set.* Sydney: Allyn & Unwin.

Perkins, K. (1981). *The mind's best work.* Cambridge, MA: Harvard University Press.

Pierce, C.S. (1931–1958). *Collected writings* (8 Volumes). C. Hartshorne, P. Weiss, & A.W. Burks (Eds). Cambridge, MA: Harvard University Press.

Pink, D. (2006). *A whole new mind: Why right-brainers will rule the future.* London: Penguin Books.

Potter, E.F., & Edens, K.M. (2001). Children's motivational beliefs about art: Exploring age differences and relation to drawing behaviour. Paper presented at the annual meeting of the American Educational Research Association, Seattle, WA, April 10–14.

Rabiger, M. (2008). *Directing: Film techniques and aesthetics* (4th ed.). Burlington, MA: Focal Press.

Rogoff, B. (1990). *Apprenticeship in thinking: Cognitive development in social contexts.* New York: Oxford University Press.

Ross, J. (2000). Arts education in the information ages: A new place for somatic wisdom. *Arts Education Review, 101*(6), 27–32.

Schaffer, H.R. (1992). Joint involvement episodes as contexts for cognitive development. In H. McGurk (Ed.), *Childhood and social development: Contemporary perspectives* (pp. 99–129). Hove: Lawrence Erlbaum.

Short, K.G., Kauffman, G., & Kahn, L.H. (2000). 'I just need to draw': Responding to literature across multiple sign systems. *The Reading Teacher, 54*(2), 160–172.

Siegel, M. (1995). More than words: The generative power of transmediation for learning. *Canadian Journal of Education, 20,* 455–475.

Slaughter, R. (1994a). *From fatalism to foresight: Educating for the early 21st Century.* Hawthorn: Australian Council for Educational Administration.

Slaughter, R. (1994b). From individual to social capacity. *Futures, 28*(8), 751–762.

Smith, N. (1982). The visual arts in early childhood education: Development and the creation of meaning. In B. Spodek (Ed.), *Handbook of research in early childhood education* (pp. 295–317). New York: Free Press.

Sternberg, R.J., & Lubart, T.I. (1995). *Defying the crowd: Cultivating creativity in a culture of conformity.* New York: Free Press.

Sutton-Smith, B. (1995). Play as performance, rhetoric, and metaphor. *Play and Culture, 2,* 189–192.

Tharpe, T. (2003). *The creative habit: Learn it and use it for life.* New York: Simon and Schuster.

Thompson, C., & Bales, S. (1991). Michael doesn't like my dinosaurs: Conversations in a pre-school art class. *Studies in Art Education, 32*(1), 43–55.

Thompson, C.H. (1995). 'What shall I draw today?' Sketchbooks in early childhood. *Art Education, 48*(5), 6–11.

Thompson, D.K. (2002). Early childhood literacy education, wakefulness, and the arts. In L. Bresler, & C.M. Thompson (Eds), *The arts in children's lives* (pp. 185–194). Netherlands: Kluwer Academic Publishers.

Tobin, J. (2000). *'Good guys don't wear hats': Children's talk about the media.* New York: Teachers College Press.

Trevarthen, C. (1995). The child's need to learn a culture. *Children in Society, 9*(1), 5–19.

UNICEF Convention on the Rights of the Child. (1989) Retrieved 6 January from www.unicef.org/crc

Van Leeuwen, T. (2005). *Introducing social semiotics.* London: Routledge.

Vygotsky, L. (1962). *Thought and language.* Cambridge, MA: MIT Press.

Vygotsky, L. (1967). Play and its role in the mental development of the child. *Soviet Psychology, 5*(3), 6–18. (1978). In J.S. Bruner, A. Jolly, & K. Sylva (Eds), *Play: Its role in development and evolution* (pp. 537–554). Harmondsworth: Penguin Books.

Vygotsky, L. (1978). *Mind in society: The development of higher psychological processes.* (M. Cole, V. John-Steiner, S. Scribner, & E. Souberman Eds). Cambridge, MA: Harvard University Press.

Wertsch, J.V. (1985). *Culture, communication and cognition: Vygotskian perspectives.* Cambridge: Cambridge University Press.

Wilson, B. (1974). The super-heroes of J.C. Holz. *Art Education, 27*(8), 2–9.

Wilson, B., & Wilson, M. (1977). An iconoclastic view of the imagery sources in the drawings of young people. *Art Education, 30,* 4–12.

Wilson, B. & Wilson, M. (1979). Children's story drawings: Reinventing worlds. *School Arts, 78*(8), 6–11.

Wolf, D., & Perry, M.D. (1988). From endpoints to repertoires: Some new conclusions about drawing development. *Journal of Aesthetic Education, 22*(1), 17–34.

Wright, S. (2001). Drawing and storytelling as a means for understanding children's concepts of the future. *Futures, 6*(2), 1–20.

Wright, S. (2003a). *The arts, young children and learning.* Boston, MA: Allyn and Bacon.

Wright, S. (2003b). Ways of knowing in the arts. In S. Wright (Ed.), *Children, meaning-making and the arts* (pp. 1–34). Frenchs Forest, NSW: Pearson Education Australia.

Wright, S. (2005). Children's multimodal meaning-making through drawing and storytelling. *Teachers College Record,* date published: 15 September 2005, ID Number: 12175. www.tcrecord.org

Wright, S. (2007a). Graphic-narrative play: Authoring through multiple texts and fluid structures. *International Journal of Education and the Arts, 8*(8), 1–27.

Wright, S. (2007b). Young children's meaning-making through drawing and 'telling': Analogies to filmic textual features. *Australian Journal of Early Childhood, 32*(4), 37–48.

Author Index

Abbs 9, 170, 176, 177, 178
Anning 7, 24, 167, 169, 174, 178
Anning and Ring 7, 24, 54
Arnheim 18
Athey 30, 65, 79, 87

Barber 81, 87, 92
Barthes 15, 56, 143, 164
Best 80
Bettelheim 141, 164
Bhroin 86
Bresler 5, 167
Brooker 26
Bruner 18, 26, 78
Buckham 11

Callery 81, 108
Campbell 141
Chandler 9, 11, 12, 15, 17, 22, 35,
    40, 45, 56, 64, 67, 80, 86,
    103, 110, 134, 167
Cox 11, 20, 22, 27, 52
Csikszentmihalyi 3

Danesi 9, 11, 12, 13, 14, 15, 31,
    82, 83, 97, 100, 140, 142, 143
Dewey 4, 10, 55, 80
Dyson 6, 10, 17, 20, 54, 112,
    135, 136

Eco 14
Egan 2, 8, 10, 11, 18, 19, 26, 45,
    61, 139, 140, 145, 164, 168
Eisner 8, 17, 178
Eckersley 10

Gadsden 2
Gallas 18, 20, 24, 29, 30
Gardner 2, 3, 18, 83, 84, 169
Geetz 22, 170
Gelb 97
Godard 134
Golomb 4, 17, 20, 27, 52, 65, 68,
    86, 112, 114, 135, 152, 153

Goodman 18, 22
Goody 140
Griffith 122
Gross 54, 79, 108

Hodge and Tripp 113
Hollyman 78, 108
Hughes 26
Hull and Nelson 2
Humphrey 80

Jakobson and Halle
    86, 140
James and Prout 26
Jewitt and Oyama 114

Kellman 10, 18
Kendrick and McKay
    20, 76
Kline 136, 144
Kolbe 27, 52
Kress 6, 8, 20, 22, 30, 82, 84, 166,
    169, 170, 178
Kress and van Leeuwen 73,
    76, 114

Labitsi 29
Lakoff and Johnson 71, 82
Lang 159
Langer 13
Leach 140
Lecoq 81
Lévi-Strauss 139, 140
Lewis 20
Linqvist 20, 83, 170
Lyons 97

MacKenzie 166
Matthews 20, 24, 30, 81,
    86, 87
Metz 45, 64

Nichols 74
Nutbrown 170, 178

Pahl and Rowsell 7, 36,
    84, 177
Paley 145
Palmer 144
Perkins 3
Pierce 30, 97
Pink 81, 82, 166, 167,
    168, 178
Potter and Edens 27

Rabiger 9, 10, 19, 84, 122, 139,
    142, 144, 145, 154, 155,
    159, 164
Rogoff 26
Ross 80

Schaffer 27, 171
Short, Kauffman and Kahn
    20, 76
Siegel 55, 76
Slaughter 10
Smith 86
Sternberg and Lubart 3
Stinson 110
Sutton-Smith 135,
    136, 144

Thompson 4, 20, 54, 175
Thompson and Bales 4
Tobin 30
Trevarthen 27

UNICEF Convention on the
    Rights of the Child 26

van Leeuwen 13, 59
Vygotsky 17, 26, 168

Wertsch 26
Wilson and Wilson 29,
    112, 168
Wolf and Perry 86
Wright 3, 4, 7, 10, 20, 29, 36,
    39, 41

Subject Index

Added to a page number 'f' denotes a figure, 't' denotes a table and 'n' denotes notes.

above/below 65, 66, 74
abstract concepts 10, 15, 172
abstract thought 20, 49, 78,
    140–1, 174
acculturation 169
action 21, 90, 173
    see also graphic action; parallel
        action; 'thinking
        in/through action'
action film 126
action lines 126–7
action representation 86
action-adventure stories 144
action-packed drawings 151, 152,
    155, 173
adult presence 27
aesthetic appreciation 4, 5t
aesthetic experience 4
aesthetic form 6, 15, 171, 172
aesthetics 157, 162, 171
affective abstraction 140
affective connections 9, 19, 99
affective development 171
after-the-event stories 47–8
agency 35–40, 50
allegory 139, 144–52, 154, 163,
    174–5
alteration 5, 18–19, 170
'anchored' meaning 56, 61, 75
animals 154
animation/audiation 64, 122
antagonists 144
anthropomorphism 150
arrows 104–6
art
    and learning 2–3
    as literacy 7, 23
    meaning-making see meaning-
        making
    and play 54–5, 172
    social purpose of 26–7
    see also child art; drawing;
        mark-making; school art
art education 2, 54
Art as Experience 10
art-making 4, 10, 27, 81
The Arts, Young Children and
    Learning 4
'assemblage of signs' 22
association 103, 143
    see also connotation
attunement 27, 28, 81, 171
audience 28, 112, 171
authentic learning 175
authentic participation 20, 170
author-artist 22, 23, 36
authorial intentions 17, 50, 113,
    163, 175
awareness 9, 17, 60–1, 81, 92

Barthes, Roland 15
Before Writing 7
before-and-after event 124
behaviour 27
Beyond 2050 147–51
'big picture' ideas 134, 173
binary concepts/oppositions 139,
    140–4, 155, 174
blended genres 110
Brecht, Bertolt 9
Bruner, Jerome 26, 78

causal schemes 19–20, 45
character dialogues 19
character-driven film 155
character-driven narratives 146–7,
    156–9, 163, 175
characters 5, 40, 44, 112, 133–4,
    138, 139, 144, 174
child art 5, 27
child development 7, 26, 27
child-as-creator/created 36, 40
child-as-subject/spectator 36
childhood 10, 26, 174
Children's Minds, Talking Rabbits
    and Clockwork Oranges 8
children's rights 5, 26
cinematic film 154–5
clarification 28
classifications 140
close/distant 65–6, 74
cognition 173
cognitive development 7, 171
collaborative, education as 176
colour(s) 82, 83, 133, 173
commitment 3
communication 6, 8, 13, 54, 55
    graphic-narrative-embodied
        17, 19, 54
    metaphorical 81, 82, 133, 170–1
    reference-based 30–5
    see also dialogue; grammar of
        communication; language(s);
        semiotics; voicing
communicative intentions 27
community 4
competence 2, 26, 30, 50, 54
complications 143–4
composition 3, 4, 5–9, 83, 170, 171
    see also free composition/ drawing
'composition in progress' 126
conception of mind 8, 17
configuration-movement
    relationship 87, 88f, 91t
configurational signs 18–19, 22,
    34, 170, 178
conformity 174
connecting icons 99, 100t, 172
    see also separating icons
connection 4, 9, 19, 99
connotation(s) 15, 16, 71, 127,
    159–60, 173
content 6, 18, 86, 171, 172
    see also form-content relationship
context 27–8
contrast(s) 82
creative play 81
creative potential 3
creative processes 5t, 23, 171
creativity 2, 3–4, 8, 11, 20, 80, 84,
    166, 167, 177
creator/created, child as 36, 40
critical thinking 10
cross-channel thinking-feeling 82
cross-cutting 122
cross-modal expressions 82
cultural activity, education as 176
cultural models 45–6
culture
    and perception 74
    see also folk culture; mass
        culture; popular culture
curriculum 7, 10, 61, 170

deep level meaning 14, 15, 172
deficit approach/model 27
denotation 15, 16
depicted/depicter 36
depth 65, 83
developmental semiotics 30
Dewey, John 4, 10
dialogue 4, 17, 19, 155, 175
'different time, different space'
    118–19
    The Olympics and the Police
        Place 119–26, 135
direction/directionality 32, 33, 90
disembodiement 167
disempowerment 169
dispositions 170, 176, 177
distance 65
dominant characters 144
dots 98–9, 100f, 100t
dramatic play 7, 19, 36, 170
dramatization 20, 83, 144
drawing
    competence in 2
    composition see composition
    creativity 2
    in early education 61
    learning through 80, 177–8
    meaning-making 11, 26, 54, 61
    teachers' perception of 177
    and writing 55
    see also visual narratives
dualism 139, 140
dynamic events 172

early childhood education 2, 11, 61
education 84, 169, 176–7
    see also art education;
        curriculum; schooling;
        teachers
educational systems 8
elaboration 5t, 18–19, 28, 29, 32
embodied imagination 170
embodied mode 21t, 37–9, 134
    see also graphic-narrative-
        embodied mode
embodiement 78–106
emergent literacy 61
emotional connection 9, 19, 99
emotions 19, 80, 81, 111, 139
empathy 19–20, 27, 80–1, 84,
    153, 168, 171, 177
empowerment 135
enactive mode 36, 40, 78, 79–96,
    102, 106–7t, 172–3
enactive skills 78, 79
event-based artwork 141–2,
    147–51
events 18, 40, 42, 44, 45, 64,
    85–6, 112
existential, education as 176
expression 4, 8, 82, 166
externalized narratives 28

fabulistic stories 134, 135
fading out/in device 121–2
fantasy 8, 10, 18, 29, 43–4, 81,
    111, 139, 146, 147, 151, 155,
    157, 162, 174
features, of artwork 27
fiction 10, 45, 111
fictional self 40, 151

figure 67
film dialogue 19
filmic features 112–19
fingers, using 90–3
first-person narration 36, 50, 172
flags 103–4
flexibility 2, 5t, 177
fluency 5t, 177
folk culture 144
foretelling 55, 73
form 6, 47, 100t
    analogies to cinematic and
        theatrical film 154–62
    and gender 152–4
    see also aesthetic form
form-content relationship
    17, 87, 126
frames 113, 114, 121, 124, 173
free composition/drawing 7, 45,
    166–7, 169
freeze frames 114–15, 116f, 173
front/behind 65–6, 74
frontality 114, 115f
function(s) 27, 50, 57, 61, 99,
    100t, 175
future-oriented values 10, 11, 24
Futures 8, 151–2, 177

gender 152–4, 159
generic concepts 41
genre(s) 6, 110
geographic model 148, 150–1
Gestalt Psychology 67
gestural marks 86–9
gesture(s) 6, 19, 85–6, 173, 178
grammar of communication 6, 171
graphic action 18, 19, 170
graphic devices 56–65, 74, 172
graphic foretelling 55, 73
graphic intentions 55
graphic mode 21t
graphic rules 67
graphic speech 17
graphic strategies 27
graphic-ing 36
graphic-narrative-embodied
    communication 17, 19, 54
graphic-narrative-embodied mode
    20, 23
graphic-narrative-embodied play
    112, 134, 135
graphic-narrative-embodied signs 6
graphic-narrative-embodied texts
    13, 74
ground 67
gustatory icons 97

'here and now' 10
hermeneutics 14–15
heroes 143, 152, 153
hidden meaning 14
high concept/high touch
    168, 169, 177
holistic texts 13, 64, 171
hooking/unhooking themes 132–3
horizontal axes 71–5

iconic devices 56–65, 74, 172
iconic mode 78, 97–102, 107t,
    172, 173
iconic skills 78
iconicity 96
icons 32, 97, 172
identification 39–40
identification indexes 31, 171
identity 36, 41
ideologies 138, 139, 154, 162, 174
imagination 2, 4, 8, 81, 84, 111,
    143, 167, 169, 170
imaginative narratives 178
imaginative universe 10

impersonal plane 151
implicit content 86
implicit interactions 64
implied dialogue 175
improvisation 4, 5–6, 17–22, 171
indexes 30–5
indexical gestures 50
indexical signs 31, 32–3, 50
indexical words 30, 31, 50, 171
inferences 34, 171
informal learning 74
insider-outsider positioning 36
integration 173
intentions/intentionality 8, 17,
    27, 50, 55, 57, 113, 163, 175
inter-connectivity 134
interactions 28, 64, 74, 172
interlocutors 25f, 28–30, 35, 41–2,
    44, 60, 176
internalized narratives 28
internalizing actions 172
interpretive space 22, 126
intertextuality 109–36, 173
intratextuality 53–76, 172
intrinsic motivation 3, 80
inventiveness 10, 11, 81, 168, 177

joint involvement episodes 27, 171
joyfulness 168, 177

kinaesthetic learning 169
knowledge
    construction 7
    see also professional knowledge;
        scientific knowledge;
        somatic knowledge

L-directed thinking 168
labels/labelling 56, 59–60, 62, 74
language(s) 22, 26, 82, 91t,
    102–3, 171
'layers of text' 14
learning 79–80, 169
    art and 2–3, 54–5
    authentic 175
    internal reorganization of
        ideas 78
    and perception 64, 71, 74
    sensorimotor 81–2
left- and right-brain capabilities 168
levels, spatial 103–4
linear texts 13
lines 83, 98–9, 100f, 100t
    see also action lines; mind lines;
        multilinearity; whoosh
        lines
linguistic competence 54
listening 42, 169
literacy/literacies 2, 7, 23, 54,
    61, 167
literal message 15, 172
location indexes 31, 32, 171
logocentric conception of mind 8
longevity 157, 162

macro text 17, 22
magic 157
mark-making 18, 54, 165
mass culture 143
meaning 177
    fantasy-based 43–4
    inferences about 171
    levels of 14–17
    spatial relations and 64–75
meaning-making 2, 6, 7, 9–22,
    23, 27
    content as 6
    in drawing 11, 26, 54, 61
    researching 30
    somatic 80, 81
medals 103–4

mediating concepts 174
memories 84
metaphorical communication
    81, 82, 133, 170–1
metaphors 19, 71, 82–3, 172
metaphysical plane 143, 174
mime 81
mimicry 81
mind lines 139
mirror neurons 80
mirror/mirroring 19, 28
mixed-media 22, 50, 61, 74
moral imperatives 142–3, 174
movement-based icons 77f, 98–9
    see also action lines; whoosh
        lines
movement-configuration
    relationship 87, 88f, 91t
multilinearity 134
multimodal acts 12, 13, 14
multimodal texts 6–7, 47, 171
    see also visual narratives
multimodality 2, 169, 176
multiple perspectives 174
multiple roles 173
multiple scenes 126–34, 173
mutually transformative processes
    20, 170
mythical plane 143, 174
Mythologies 143
myth(s) 111, 139, 140, 142–3

names/naming 57–9, 61, 74
narrative mode 21t
    see also graphic-narrative-
        embodied mode
narratives 18, 36
    see also visual narratives
neurological research 80
new literacies 2
nudging probes 28, 29
numbers 104–6

objectivity 5t
objects 9, 18, 40, 44, 64, 112, 173
olfactory icons 97
The Olympics and the Police
    Place 119–26, 135
omniscient narrator 127, 151
onomatopoeia 99, 100–2
oral storytelling 139, 174
organizational indexes 31
orientation 71–5, 173
orientation-based indexes 34–5
orientational metaphors 71
other-wordliness 18, 20, 29, 43,
    44, 111, 135, 173
outloud thinking 28

parable 145
parallel action 122, 126
parents 4, 74
participation 4, 20, 28–9, 36, 170
pedagogy 10, 26, 170, 176
people 18, 64
perception 4, 6, 64, 67, 71, 74, 86,
    97, 171
perceptual-physical acts 87
performance 81
personality traits 3
personalized narrative 46
personalized theories 140, 162, 174
perspective(s) 65, 83, 174
photo-shoot drawings 114, 173
Picasso 2
place(s) 6, 18, 64, 112
planners 4
play 8, 18, 19, 21, 26, 54–5, 80,
    81, 172
    see also dramatic play; graphic-
        narrative-embodied play

playfulness 80, 102
plot development 138
plot points 144
plot-driven film 155
plot-driven narratives 163, 175
plots 5, 19, 174
polyvocality 40–1
popular culture 143
popular media 45, 110, 111, 139, 141, 142, 151, 162, 173
possibility 9, 10
predisposition, and perception 64, 71, 74
preferability 10
problem setting/solving 4, 5t, 112
processes of production 17
production 4, 17, 171
professional knowledge 170
prototypes 41–5, 50, 120
prototypicality 40, 127, 135, 146, 151, 172
proximity 67–71, 74, 172
psychosomatic awareness 92
purpose(s) 27, 100t

quasi-human figures 145, 146, 147, 163, 175

R-directed thinking 168
radiating lines 63
radiational thoughts/feelings 18, 29, 134
real-time graphic-ing 18, 47, 55, 170
reality 9, 10, 11, 17, 29, 45, 80, 111
reciprocity 27, 28, 171
reference-based communication 30–5
referring 103
reflective probe 28
relationships 3, 6, 112
    see also configuration-movement relationship; form-content relationship; spatial relations
repeated words 99, 100–2
repetition 79, 110
representation 2, 9, 12, 14, 27, 81
re-visioning 4, 9, 173
rhyme 59
rituals 143
rule-bound 6, 7, 23, 169, 171, 177
rules 2, 67

'same space, different time' 117
'same time, different space' 118
'same time, same space' 114–17
    See also different time,different place
scene(s) 113, 126–34, 173
schemas 6, 18, 79–80
school art 174
schooling 7, 23, 84, 166–7, 169, 177, 178
scientific knowledge 148–50
selectivity 5t
self-realization 175
Semi-Taxi and Sky Patrol 109, 127–34
semiotic dispositions 170, 176
semiotic modalities 12
semiotic units 14, 17
semiotics 11–12, 22, 30, 103, 168
    see also sign systems; signing/sign making; signs
sense memory 84
sensitive participation 28–9
sensorimotor learning 81–2
sensorimotor thinking 80, 171
sensory mirror neurons 80
sensory-based issues 37–9, 157, 162

sensory-kinaesthetic icons 97
separating icons 99, 100t, 172
    see also conneting icons
sequences 46–7, 73, 113, 124
shapes 83
shot (filmic) 113, 114
sign systems 14, 178
signified 14, 16
signifiers 14, 15, 16
signifying practices 11–12, 171
signing/sign-making 22, 170, 172
signs 6, 12–13, 22, 59, 138
    see also configurational signs; indexical signs; prototypes; symbols
silences, in narratives 19, 30
silent narration 55
similarity 67–71, 74, 172
skills 177
'small' signs 13, 15, 56, 171
social constructionist/ constructivist pedagogies 26
social development 7
social semiotics 103
socio-cultural perspectives 26
somatic knowledge 80, 81, 171
somatic meaning-making 80, 81
sound 173
space 82, 113–19, 124, 173
spatial relations 64–75, 138, 171
speech 6, 17, 56, 74, 112
speech bubbles 57, 62, 64, 74, 172
stereotypes 3
stories 18, 126, 172
storyboard 117n
storying 45, 47–8
storytelling 6–7, 18, 138, 139, 174
structural perception 71
structure 6, 18, 110, 112, 113, 134, 139, 173
stylization 159–62
subject, child as 36
subtexts 138, 142, 174
surface level meaning 14, 15, 172
surrogate emotional experience 9, 139
surroundedness 67, 68–71, 74, 172
suspense 143
suspension of disbelief 29, 36–7, 44, 171
symbol weaving 55
symbolic form 171
symbolic message 15, 172
symbolic mode 10, 73, 78, 102–6, 107t, 173
symbolic representation 54
symbolic skills 78
symbolic world 9, 171
symbols 9, 57, 102–3, 171
synaesthesia 83, 84, 169, 172
syntagm 64n
syntagmatic spatial relations 64–75
systems of conventions 14

tactile icons 97
teachers/educators 4, 10, 11, 24, 166, 170, 176, 177
temporal indexes 31, 171
temporal sequences 46–7, 73
tension(s) 138, 139, 142, 143, 147
texts 2, 13
    see also holistic texts; intertextuality; intratextuality; layers of text; multimodal texts; subtexts
texture 83
theatric features 112–19
theatrical film 155–9

thinking
    children's 18, 26, 29, 54
    L- and R-directed 168
    modes see enactive mode; iconic mode; symbolic mode
    sensorimotor 80, 171
    styles 3
    see also abstract thought; binary concepts/oppositions; cognition; critical thinking; outloud thinking; schemas
'thinking in/through action' 20, 78, 134, 170
third-person narration 36, 46, 50, 151, 172
time 6, 82, 113–19, 124, 173
    see also temporal indexes; temporal sequences
topics
    engagement in unfamiliar 8
    gender and self-selected 152–4, 175
tracking shot 127
traffic lights 104–6
transformation 5t, 6, 16–17, 36, 38, 80, 97, 177
transformative processes 20, 170

UN Convention on the Rights of the Child 26
uniforms 103–4
universal concepts/themes 41, 45–50, 144

value, contrast portrayal 82
values 10, 11, 24, 50, 169, 175
vector-based depictions 114, 115f, 172
vertical axes 71–5
visual learning 169
visual metaphors 82–3, 172
visual narratives, and embodiement 78–106
visual narratives 17–22
    agency and polyvocality 35–50
    enactive engagement 78
    intertextuality 109–36
    intratextuality 53–76
    levels of meaning 15
    signs as prototypes 41–5
    structure 6, 18
    turning experience or universal themes into 45–50
    variation in sophistication 74–5
visual perception 4, 6, 64, 67, 74, 86, 97, 171.
visual symbols 103
visual-motor creating 87
vocalisms 21, 28, 60, 81, 100, 172, 178
voicing 57, 151, 172
    see also speech; speech bubbles
Vygotsky, Lev 17, 26, 168

wavy lines 63
A whole new mind: why right-brainers will rule the future 166
whoosh lines 19, 56, 63–4, 74, 86, 98, 134, 172
words
    interplay between images and 57
    see also indexical words; onomatopoeia; repeated words
writing 55

zebra crossings 104–6